MAY 2016

DISCARD

Clodagh's
Irish
Kitchen

Clodagh's
Irish
Kitchen

Clodagh McKenna

Photography by Tara Fisher

Kyle Books

For my Dad
I would give up everything to share one more meal with you

Published in 2015 by Kyle Books
www.kylebooks.com
general.enquiries@kylebooks.com

Distributed by National Book Network
4501 Forbes Blvd., Suite 200
Lanham, MD 20706
Phone: (800) 462-6420
Fax: (800) 338-4550
customercare@nbnbooks.com

Published in Great Britain by
Kyle Books, an imprint of Kyle Cathie Ltd

10 9 8 7 6 5 4 3 2

ISBN 978-1-909487-29-1

Editor: Tara O'Sullivan
Designer: Lucy Gowans
Photographer: Tara Fisher
Food Stylists: Annie Rigg and Kathryn Bruton
Prop Stylist: Wei Tang
Americanizer: Jo Richardson
Production: Nic Jones and Gemma John

Library of Congress Control Number: 2014958254

Color reproduction by ALTA London
Printed and bound in China by C&C Offset Printing
Co., Ltd.

My Irish Kitchen

When I told non-Irish people that I was writing this book, their answer was always: "Really? What is modern Irish cuisine?"

For me, it can be summed up as clean-tasting, fresh dishes using light subtle flavors to encourage the main ingredients, whether they are fresh fish, aged beef, mountain lamb or herb-flavored creamy sauces and butter. Wild foraged foods, such as nettles, samphire, elderflowers and so on have become commonplace in Irish cuisine. Our island has a rugged western coastline that is sprayed with Atlantic ocean waves every day, salting the pastures and giving us some of the most fantastic food in the world. Where else can you drive along a road and be stopped by sheep crossing in front of you while wild blackberries tumble out of the hedgerows on either side and samphire and seaweeds scatter the nearby shores? Our sheep and cows graze on herby and floral pastures, creating beautiful meats, milk, cream, butter and cheeses and our clean tidal waters are a natural habitat for fantastic seafood. We have always had all the bases of a rich and varied cuisine—what we were missing was the know-how to make the most of it.

The Irish kitchen and the Irish palate has evolved so much over the past ten years or so. There are many contributing factors to this. Irish people that have lived abroad (including myself) have come back with inspirational ideas from the

Our island has a rugged western coastline that is sprayed with Atlantic ocean waves every day, salting the pastures and giving us some of the most fantastic food in the world

restaurants and food markets they found on their travels. The recession in Ireland has also played a surprisingly positive role, as Irish people have become more aware of the importance of supporting our local farmers, fishermen and food producers. This has a domino effect, as it enables the suppliers to expand their offerings, and experiment with creating new products that previously we may have imported, such as fresh buffalo mozzarella, which is now made in Toonsbridge Dairy in County Cork. The domino effect then continues onto the plates in Irish restaurants, and finally into Irish homes. The increasing number of farmers' markets

My influences are pulled from the wonderful places I have visited and the ingredients of the country I call home.

around the country have not only opened another gate for buying fresh, local ingredients, but have also encouraged direct communication between the cook and the fisherman, farmer and producer.

My influences are pulled from the wonderful places I have visited and the ingredients of the country I call home. When I lived in Italy and France, I discovered many fantastic recipes, and they became a part of my Irish kitchen when I returned home. I altered them, however, to make the most of the great produce that we have here in Ireland—the classic Italian dish gnocchi, for example, evolved into my Wild Nettle Gnocchi with Cashel Blue Sauce (page 134), and I tweaked a recipe for fresh pasta to include dillisk, a beautiful red Irish seaweed (page 138). I'm inspired every time I look out to our seas, walk our shores or drive along the country roads of Ireland, and this is reflected in my cooking, from my risotto made delicious and sweet with Dublin Bay Prawns (page 136), or Summer Lamb with Fennel and Roasted Nectarines (page 147).

I'm inspired every time I look out to our seas, walk our shores or drive along the country roads of Ireland, and this is reflected in my cooking.

You will also find some more traditional Irish recipes in this book that I have held on to because they are just so good–a lot of them I would call Irish "soul food," because they belong with a memory and warm my soul when I cook them. These include the traditional Irish Lamb Stew with Pearl Barley (page 82) and of course the classic Beef and Guinness Pie (page 98), although even this recipe has been updated and enhanced with the addition of a little grated dark chocolate to the rich sauce. So even the most traditional of dishes have evolved over time, becoming part of the fabric of modern Ireland. You see, in Ireland, life revolves around the kitchen, whether it's cups of tea and a piece of cake fresh from the range, a family supper, Sunday lunch, or our famed Irish breakfast–life happens over a simmering pot in Ireland. When you are welcomed into an Irish home, the first thing that happens is the kettle is put on, and you are asked "Are you hungry?" Sunday lunch is as much a tradition as going to mass on a Sunday morning, and when there is a celebration or loss in a family, it's food we turn to for comfort and joy. Perhaps it's a Catholic thing–we may have taken the loaves and fishes to heart!

My kitchen in Ireland has become an experimental haven for me, a place where I create recipes for my restaurants, articles, television, Aer Lingus flight menus and this book. And that's why the name *Clodagh's Irish Kitchen* came so naturally to my mind. As you flip through the pages, my wish is that Irish cuisine will become part of your kitchen, and that many of the older recipes that have been handed down to me will become a tradition in your family too. Most of all I would like this book to create a table full of happy faces and heart-warming moments, because that's the greatest gift life gives you through food.

WEEKEND *Baking*

Health Loaf Bread

I am the third generation in my family that bakes this health loaf recipe, and I hope that it continues for many generations after me. The recipe originated from my father's mother, Kathleen McKenna. Then my father's sister Muriel started baking it, and when she would visit she would always come with a loaf of this bread as a gift. It's a fantastic bread, full of fiber.

1 Preheat the oven to 450°F. Lightly grease two 5x9-inch loaf pans and dust with wheat germ.

2 Pour all the dry ingredients into a large bowl and mix together.

3 Make a well in the center of the dry ingredients and, using a wooden spoon, gradually stir in the buttermilk, until a moist dough forms.

4 Divide the dough between the prepared loaf pans. Smooth the tops and, using a floured knife, make a large cross on each one. Sprinkle with the remaining wheat germ and sesame and pumpkin seeds.

5 Place in the oven and bake for 8 to 10 minutes, then reduce the heat to 275°F and bake for another hour.

6 Remove the loaves from the oven and let cool in the pans for a few minutes, then turn out onto a wire rack and let cool completely.

The loaves will keep for up to 1 week in an airtight container.

Makes 2 loaves

vegetable oil, for greasing
3½ cups whole-wheat flour
½ cup wheat germ, plus more for dusting
½ cup all-purpose flour, plus more for flouring
1 cup wheat bran
scant ½ cup ground flaxseed
1 tablespoon spirulina powder
1⅓ cups steel cut oatmeal
2 teaspoons brown sugar
2½ teaspoons baking soda
4¼ cups buttermilk

For the topping
2 teaspoons (1 per loaf) wheat germ
2 teaspoons (1 per loaf) sesame seeds
2 teaspoons (1 per loaf) pumpkin seeds

Thyme-Herbed Soda Bread

Soda bread to Ireland is what pasta is to Italy. It is as Irish as the flag itself!
Every Irish kitchen has been filled with the aroma of freshly baked Irish soda
bread, which is light and crumbly in texture, with a soft richness that comes
from the buttermilk. You can make it with regular milk if you are unable to get
your hands on buttermilk. The fresh thyme adds a light floral aroma, but it's
a delicate flavor. You can also substitute the thyme for rosemary, 1 teaspoon
ground fennel seeds or $1/3$ cup raisins.

1 Preheat the oven to 425°F. Flour a baking sheet and set aside.

2 Sift the flours, followed by the baking soda, into a large mixing
bowl and add a pinch of salt, and the thyme. Mix together with
clean hands.

3 Make a well in the center of the flour mixture and slowly pour
the buttermilk into the well. Use your free hand to mix the flour
into the buttermilk–try to spread your fingers far apart so that your
hand resembles a trough. Make sure there are no dry patches and
that the dough is completely wet.

4 Flour your hands and shape the dough into a round. Place on
the floured baking sheet. Flour a large knife and cut the shape of a
cross into the top of the dough, two-thirds of the way through, and
then stab every quarter with the knife. This old Irish tradition was
apparently to kill the fairies! Using a pastry brush, brush the round
of bread with the remaining buttermilk–this will give the bread a
lovely color once baked.

5 Bake in the oven for about 25 minutes, then turn the bread over
and bake for another 5 minutes. To test whether the loaf is cooked,
tap the bottom with your knuckles–it should sound hollow.

6 Cool on a wire rack before serving.

The soda bread will keep for 3 to 4 days in an airtight container.

Makes 1 large loaf

$3^{1}/4$ cups whole-wheat flour
$3^{2}/3$ cups all-purpose flour, plus
   extra for flouring
$1^{1}/2$ teaspoons baking soda
pinch of sea salt
1 tablespoon finely chopped thyme
$2^{1}/2$ cups buttermilk, plus
   3 tablespoons for brushing

Cheese and Rosemary Savory Scones

I love serving these scones alongside a soup as a starter or light lunch dish. You could make mini scones by halving the size of the scones, which would be lovely placed on your guests' side plates when hosting a dinner party. There are so many variations: olives and sun-blushed tomatoes, thyme and parmesan, pancetta and basil, or blue cheese and walnuts. You can make the dough the night before and bake the following day just before serving them, as they are at their finest when eaten on the day they are baked.

1 Preheat the oven to 400°F. Grease a baking sheet with oil and set aside.

2 Sift the flour, baking powder, and salt into a large bowl. Using your fingertips, rub the butter into the flour mixture, until it resembles fine bread crumbs. Stir in two-thirds of the shredded cheese, followed by the rosemary. Gradually mix in enough milk to make a soft dough.

3 On a floured work surface, roll out the dough to a thickness of ½ inch. Using a cookie cutter or an upturned glass measuring 2 inches, cut the dough into circles. Place on the oiled baking sheet and sprinkle the remaining cheese on top.

4 Bake in the oven for 12 to 15 minutes, until golden.

5 Transfer to a wire rack and let cool for 15 minutes before serving.

The scones will keep for up to 3 days in an airtight container, but are best eaten on the day they are made.

Makes 8 scones

oil, for greasing
1¾ cups all-purpose flour, plus more for flouring
1 tablespoon baking powder
a pinch of sea salt
3½ tablespoons butter, chilled and cubed
1 cup shredded sharp Irish cheddar cheese, such as Hegarty's or Bandon Vale
2 teaspoons finely chopped rosemary
½ to ⅔ cup milk

Soda Bread Farls

This recipe is a very traditional way of making bread and it's a really quick method–great for those unexpected guests! The dough is flattened into a circle, then cut into quarters and cooked on a dry griddle or frying pan. It was traditionally baked on a grill pan over an open fire, so it's a great way to make bread if you are camping! The bread is light with a tangy flavor from the yogurt. You could serve it alongside my Full Irish Breakfast (see page 67) or with soup, or have it toasted with butter and jam.

1 Sift the flour and baking soda into a large bowl. Pour in the milk and the yogurt (strange, I know, but it works), and mix with a spatula until you have a soft, dry dough.

2 You can shape the farls as you please, but the traditional way is to form the dough into a ball and then roll it out into a circle just under ½ inch thick, then divide into quarters.

3 Place a heavy-bottomed skillet over medium heat and sprinkle lightly with flour. When the flour starts to brown, place a farl in the pan and cook until lightly browned, 5 to 6 minutes per side. Remove the farl, sprinkle some more flour into the pan, and cook the rest in the same way. Keep in a warm place until you are ready to eat them.

Makes 4 farls

3¼ cups all-purpose flour, plus
   more for sprinkling
1 teaspoon baking soda
¾ cup milk
½ cup plain yogurt

Rosemary and Sea Salt Oatcakes

These savory oatcakes, or crackers, are light and crumbly, sweetened with fresh rosemary and salted with crunchy sea salt. They are perfect to serve with all types of cheese. You could substitute the rosemary for fresh thyme or ground fennel seeds. They also make lovely edible gifts, wrapped in parchment paper or placed in cellophane bags and tied with string or ribbons with a sprig of rosemary through the knot.

1 Preheat the oven to 350°F. Sprinkle some flour on two baking sheets.

2 Dissolve the baking powder in ¾ cup warm water and whisk in the melted butter.

3 In a large bowl, mix together the oats, flour, rosemary, salt, and sugar.

4 Pour the liquid into the dry ingredients, stirring as you pour, and mix to make a stiff dough.

5 Lightly flour a clean work surface and roll out the dough to about ¼ inch thick. Using a 2½-inch cookie cutter, cut out 30 circles.

6 Arrange the oatcakes on the prepared baking sheets and bake for 35 minutes, turning after 25 minutes, until pale golden. Cool on a wire rack before serving.

The oatcakes will keep for up to 1 week in an airtight container.

Makes 30 oatcakes

¼ teaspoon baking powder

⅓ cup butter, melted

2⅔ cups rolled oats

½ cup plus 1 tablespoon whole-wheat flour, plus extra for flouring

3 teaspoons finely chopped fresh rosemary

1 teaspoon sea salt, plus extra for sprinkling

1 tablespoon plus 1 heaping teaspoon superfine sugar

Chocolate Biscuit Cake

Ask any Irish person if they have had this cake at one stage of their childhood and the answer will probably be yes. I am not entirely sure why it is such a popular cake in Ireland – maybe because rich tea biscuits were a staple in most cookie tins in Irish households in the 1980s – but walk into any farmers' market in Ireland and you are guaranteed to find biscuit cake at every baking stall. To give this recipe more of a kick, soak the raisins in whiskey (or brandy – yes, we love brandy in Ireland too!) overnight in a fridge, drain the excess liquid from the raisins the following day and follow the recipe below. This biscuit cake is delicious served with a pot of Irish tea, any time of the day…

1 Lightly butter a 9-inch square cake pan.

2 In a glass bowl set over a saucepan of simmering water, combine the butter, syrup, and chocolate, stirring until melted and smooth.

3 Crush the cookies, but leave some slightly larger chunks. Add to the melted mixture with the raisins and hazelnuts and mix well.

4 Tip the batter into the prepared pan and press down. Let cool, then cover with plastic wrap and chill in the refrigerator until set. Cut into squares.

This will keep for up to 5 days in an airtight container.

Makes 24–30 squares

1½ sticks unsalted butter, plus more for greasing

2 tablespoons golden syrup or maple syrup

9 ounces unsweetened chocolate (70 percent cocoa solids), broken into pieces

10 ounces rich tea English biscuits or graham crackers

½ cup raisins

2/3 cup roasted skinned hazelnuts, chopped

Irish Coffee Cookies

These are what I would call "adult" cookies–and we do deserve to have our own special cookies! The whiskey raisins are utterly delicious, but if you wanted to leave out the whiskey syrup, just skip step 1. You could use semisweet or milk chocolate instead of the white, and, if you prefer, you can use hazelnuts, almonds, or pine nuts instead of the macadamia nuts.

1 Preheat the oven to 350°F and line a baking sheet with parchment paper.

2 Start by preparing the whiskey raisins: In a small saucepan, combine the raisins, whiskey, and sugar with $^1/_3$ cup plus 1 tablespoon water. Bring to a boil, cover, then reduce the heat and simmer for 20 minutes. Remove the pan from the heat, let cool, then strain the raisins, discarding the whiskey syrup.

3 Make the cookie dough: In a bowl, beat together the butter and sugars until light and fluffy. Then beat in the egg, followed by the coffee granules and vanilla extract.

4 Sift the flour, baking soda, and baking powder into the batter, and beat until the dough comes together. Fold in the whiskey raisins, chocolate, and nuts.

5 Using your hands, form the cookie dough into small, walnut-size balls and place on the lined baking sheet. Flatten out the balls into 2-inch disks using the back of a spoon. Leave about 2¾ inches between each cookie, as they will expand quite a bit when they are cooking.

6 Bake for 15 to 20 minutes, or until golden brown. Transfer to a wire rack and let cool completely.

The cookies will keep for up to 1 week in an airtight container.

Makes 16 cookies

1 stick butter, softened
¾ cup packed light brown sugar
¼ cup plus 1 tablespoon superfine sugar
1 large free-range egg
1 teaspoon ground coffee granules
1 teaspoon vanilla extract
2 cups plus 1 heaping tablespoon all-purpose flour
½ teaspoon baking soda
½ teaspoon baking powder
8 ounces white chocolate buttons (or broken bits)
1$^1/_3$ cups macadamia nuts, toasted and chopped

For the whiskey raisins
scant ½ cup raisins
3 tablespoons Irish whiskey
1 tablespoon sugar

Lavender Shortbread

The addition of lavender to the otherwise traditional shortbread is exquisite…
The lavender brings a light floral flavor that perfectly complements the buttery
shortbread. In my restaurants, we serve this as part of an afternoon tea, so
you can now create your own afternoon treat at home. For this recipe, you'll
need to start in advance as the dough requires chilling for at least 2 hours, but
preferably overnight.

1 Prepare the shortbread dough: Remove the lavender leaves from
the stems, tip them into a food processor with the brown sugar, and
blitz until well combined. Transfer to a bowl and set aside.

2 Place the butter in the food processor together with $^1/_3$ cup of the
white sugar and blitz until soft and light.

3 Gradually add the flour to the food processor, followed by the
lavender/sugar mix, and blitz again until a dough forms.

4 Turn onto a floured work surface and shape into a sausage
approximately 2 inches in diameter. Wrap tightly in aluminum foil
or plastic wrap and refrigerate for 2 hours or overnight.

5 When ready to bake: Preheat the oven to 375°F and grease a
cookie sheet with butter.

6 Using a sharp knife, slice the dough into disks approximately
$^1/_4$ inch thick and place on the prepared cookie sheet. Bake for
8 to 10 minutes, until pale golden in color.

7 Transfer to a wire rack, sprinkle with the remaining sugar, and
let cool.

The shortbread will keep for up to 1 week in an airtight container.

Makes 24 cookies

4 sprigs of dried lavender
2 tablespoons Demerara sugar
1¼ sticks plus 1 tablespoon unsalted
   butter, cubed, plus more for
   greasing
½ cup superfine sugar
1½ cups plus 1 tablespoon
   all-purpose flour

Orange Blossom Buttermilk Scones

I adore the flavor of orange blossom, especially in light, fluffy scones–it's a little bit of decadence that we can all enjoy. Don't skip the glaze, as this really is not to be missed! If you're not a fan of orange blossom, you can omit it, or replace it with vanilla extract, rosewater or lemon juice. If you can't get hold of buttermilk, use regular whole milk.

1 Preheat the oven to 425°F. Prepare a baking sheet by dredging with flour and shaking off any excess.

2 Sift the flour and baking powder into a large mixing bowl. Lightly stir in the salt.

3 Using your fingertips, rub the chilled butter into the flour, then stir in the sugar.

4 In a small bowl, mix the orange blossom water, orange zest, egg, and buttermilk. Make a well in the center of the flour mixture and gradually stir in the liquid. Try not to overstir the dough, as this will make it tough. The dough should be slightly sticky to the touch.

5 Tip the dough out onto a lightly floured work surface and gently knead, just enough to get rid of any cracks in the dough.

6 Roll the dough out to a 1-inch thickness. Using a 2-inch cookie cutter, cut out 12 circles. Lift onto the prepared baking sheet and bake in the oven for 10 to 15 minutes, until golden and risen. Cool on a wire rack.

7 While the scones are cooling, make the glaze (optional): Place the butter, sugar, and orange zest and juice in a saucepan over medium heat. Stir until the butter and sugar have melted and thickened. Then remove from the heat and, using an immersion blender, blend for 1 minute, until smooth and slightly cooled. Using a pastry brush, glaze the tops of the orange blossom scones.

The scones are best eaten on the day they are made, but will keep for up to 3 days in an airtight container.

Makes 12 scones

$3^2/_3$ cups all-purpose flour, plus more for flouring
1 teaspoon baking powder
pinch of salt
7 tablespoons unsalted butter, chilled and cubed
5 tablespoons superfine sugar
1 tablespoon orange blossom water
zest of 1 orange
1 large egg
1 cup buttermilk

For the glaze (optional)
2 tablespoons unsalted butter
1¼ cups superfine sugar
zest and juice of 2 oranges

These scones are delicious served with Orange Blossom Mascarpone Simply mix the following ingredients together:
1 tablespoon orange blossom water
1 tablespoon clear honey
1 cup mascarpone cheese

Oat, Apple and Blackberry *Muffins*

We make these in my restaurants over the autumn months, as the blackberries and apples are at their finest at that time of year in Ireland. They are lovely for breakfast or as a mid-morning snack and make a great lunchbox filler for children. You could substitute the blackberries for blueberries or raspberries.

1 Preheat the oven to 400°F. Line a muffin pan with 10 muffin liners.

2 Using a stand or handheld electric mixer, cream the butter and sugar until light and fluffy, then gradually add the eggs and milk and beat in.

3 Sift the flour and baking powder into the creamed mixture and stir in. Next add the oats, grated apples, half of the blackberries, and the cinnamon. Stir to combine.

4 Spoon the batter into the muffin liners, filling each to just over halfway. Stud each muffin with 2 or 3 blackberries and sprinkle the extra oats on top.

5 Bake in the oven for 20 minutes, or until golden on top. Remove from the oven and let cool in the pan for 5 minutes, then transfer to a wire rack and cool completely.

These muffins will keep for 3 to 4 days in an airtight container.

Makes 10 muffins

1¼ sticks plus 1 tablespoon unsalted butter
⅓ cup plus 1 tablespoon packed light brown sugar
2 eggs
⅔ cup milk
1½ cups plus 1 tablespoon all-purpose flour
2 teaspoons baking powder
1 heaping cup old-fashioned rolled oats, plus 1 tablespoon for topping
2 cooking apples, peeled, cored, and grated
1 cup fresh blackberries
1 teaspoon ground cinnamon

Cinnamon and Nutmeg *Rock Buns*

As a child, I was lucky enough to wake up every Saturday morning to the smell of these cinnamon and nutmeg rock buns wafting through the house–it was like a siren luring me from my bed to the kitchen, where my older sisters, Mairead and Niamh, would be baking with my mum. My brother Jim and I would stand around impatiently waiting for the rock buns to make their way out of the oven and onto the kitchen table. We could never wait for them to cool, and so we would tear them open and fill them with lashings of Irish butter that would melt down our fingers as we ate them with dreamy delight… I hope that these will become a Saturday ritial for you too, and fill your house with not just delicious smells but wonderful memories too.

1 Preheat the oven to 400°F. Grease a baking sheet with butter and set aside.

2 Sift the flour and baking powder into a large mixing bowl.

3 Using your fingertips, rub the cubed chilled butter into the flour until the mixture resembles bread crumbs. Using a wooden spoon, mix in the brown sugar, currants, cherries, peel, nutmeg, and cinnamon.

4 Lightly beat the egg with the milk and pour over the dry ingredients. Mix in with a fork to form a stiff batter. Place 12 rough heaps of the batter on the prepared baking sheet.

5 In a small bowl, combine the superfine sugar and cinnamon. Sprinkle the cinnamon sugar over the buns.

6 Bake in the oven for 15 minutes or until golden on top. Transfer to a wire rack and let cool.

These buns will keep for 3 to 4 days in an airtight container.

Makes 12 buns

1½ cups cake flour
1 teaspoon baking powder
1 stick unsalted butter, cubed and
    chilled, plus more for greasing
½ cup packed light brown sugar
heaping ½ cup dried currants
1 tablespoon chopped candied
    cherries
1 tablespoon chopped candied
    citrus peel
¼ teaspoon ground nutmeg
½ teaspoon ground cinnamon
1 large egg
a splash of milk

For the topping
2 tablespoons superfine sugar
½ teaspoon ground cinnamon

Chester Cake

This is also known as Gur cake in Dublin, but I grew up in County Cork and we called it Chester Cake. The recipe originated in bakeries across the county to use up the leftovers of other cakes that didn't sell. The filling is rich and dark, using leftover cake or stale bread, tea, brown sugar and fruits. I have added a light, fluffy vanilla icing to balance the richness of the cake, which I think makes it even more delicious. You can add puréed dates to the filling or substitute the golden raisins with dried cranberries at Christmas time.

1 Preheat the oven to 375°F. Grease a 12-inch square shallow baking pan with butter.

2 In a food processor, blend the stale bread or cake until you get fine crumbs. Transfer to a mixing bowl and cover with the cold tea. Let soak while you prepare the other ingredients.

3 Sift the flour and baking powder into a large mixing bowl and stir in the sugar. Using your fingertips, rub in the butter. Next, stir in the cinnamon, ginger, and lemon zest, followed by the syrup.

4 Drain any excess tea from the bread or cake crumbs and squeeze dry using your hands or the back of a wooden spoon. Bit by bit, mix the crumbs into the flour mixture, followed by the golden raisins. Lastly, mix in the milk and beaten egg, then set aside.

5 Remove the pie dough from the refrigerator and cut in half. On a lightly floured work surface, roll out one half of the dough to fit the prepared baking pan. Spoon the batter into the pastry shell and smooth it out evenly. Roll out the second half of the dough and cover the batter. Prick the top of the pastry with a knife, and bake in the oven for an hour.

6 While the cake is baking, make the frosting: Using a handheld electric mixer, beat all the ingredients until light and fluffy.

7 Once the cake is baked, remove from the oven and let cool completely in the pan, then spread the frosting on top.

The cake will keep for up to 1 week in an airtight container.

Serves 8

10½ ounces stale white bread
    or cake
1 cup cold Irish breakfast tea
1 cup all-purpose flour, plus more
    for flouring
1 tablespoon baking powder
½ cup light brown sugar
3½ tablespoons unsalted butter,
    chilled and cubed, plus more for
    greasing
¼ teaspoon ground cinnamon
¼ teaspoon ground ginger
zest of 1 lemon
$^{1}/_{3}$ cup plus 1 tablespoon golden
    syrup or dark corn syrup
1¼ cups golden raisins
$^{2}/_{3}$ cup milk
1 large egg, beaten
9 ounces pie dough, chilled

For the frosting
3½ tablespoons unsalted butter,
    softened
2 cups sifted confectioners' sugar
1 teaspoon vanilla extract
¾ cup plus 2 tablespoons cream
    cheese (not low-fat)

Irish Tea Brack

At least once every month I will bake a tea brack at home. It is possibly one of the easiest and most satisfying recipes to make. You do have to soak the fruits for a few hours, or overnight, but the rest is just weighing and mixing together. It's delicious fresh on the day it's made but, to be honest, I prefer it a couple of days later, toasted with butter and jam… The cake is dense and moist – a real crowd pleaser!

1 Place the dried fruits in a bowl and cover with the cold tea. Let soak for 3 to 4 hours.

2 Preheat the oven to 350°F. Grease a 5x9-inch loaf pan with butter.

3 In a mixing bowl, beat the sugar and egg until light and foamy. Sift in the flour, baking powder, and spices and mix together.

4 Add the soaked fruits and any remaining tea to the bowl and mix together well.

5 Transfer the batter to the greased loaf pan and bake in the oven for 1 hour.

6 Unmold and cool on a wire rack.

This loaf will keep for up to 1 week in an airtight container.

Makes 1 loaf

2^1/$_3$ cups mixed dried fruits, such as raisins, golden raisins, cherries, and currants
1 cup cold Irish breakfast tea
butter, for greasing
½ cup plus 1 tablespoon packed light brown sugar
1 large egg, beaten
2 cups all-purpose flour
2 teaspoons baking powder
2 teaspoons ground allspice, cinnamon, or nutmeg

Honey and Ginger Flapjacks

These are pretty healthy, very easy to make and so delicious with a cup of tea! They also make great lunchbox treats for kids. You could add golden raisins, dried cranberries or dried blueberrries to this recipe if you wish.

1 Preheat the oven to 300°F and line an 8-inch square shallow baking pan with parchment paper.

2 In a saucepan, place the butter, sugar, and honey over low heat and stir until melted. Remove from the heat, stir in the oats and ground and candied ginger, and mix well.

3 Spoon the mixture into the lined pan, spreading out evenly with the back of a spoon.

4 Place in the oven and bake for 45 minutes.

5 Remove from the oven and let cool for 10 minutes in the pan, then transfer to a wire rack to cool completely.

6 Cut into squares of the desired size.

These flapjacks will keep for up to 1 week in an airtight container.

Makes 18–20

7 tablespoons butter
¼ cup packed light brown sugar
3½ tablespoons golden honey
2¼ cups old-fashioned rolled oats
1 teaspoon ground ginger
¼ cup candied ginger, finely
   chopped

Barmbrack Irish Halloween Bread

Barmbrack is one of the biggest traditions of Halloween in Ireland. Traditionally, when making this cake, you add a pea, a stick, a piece of cloth, a small coin and a ring. If a person finds the pea in their slice, it means that they will not marry that year; the stick signifies an unhappy marriage; the cloth means the person will have bad luck or be poor; the coin means the person will enjoy good fortune or be rich; and the ring means the person will be wed within the year! It's a light fruitcake bread, quite different from a tea brack. After a few days it's delicious toasted and smeared with butter and raspberry jam.

1 Place the dried fruits and citrus peel in a large bowl and pour over the tea. Let the tea soak into the fruits and peel for 2 hours.

2 Sift the flour and spices into a large mixing bowl. Using your fingertips, rub the butter into the flour.

3 Warm the milk in a saucepan. Place the yeast and sugar in a measuring cup (or small bowl) and slowly whisk in the warmed milk, followed by one of the beaten eggs.

4 Make a well in the center of the flour mixture and pour the yeast liquid into the well, gradually mixing in the flour from the sides with a wooden spoon. Stir in the fruits, peel, and tea and mix well.

5 Sprinkle some flour on a board and transfer the dough onto the board. Knead gently, adding more flour if needed (the dough should be smooth but not sticky). Transfer the dough to a lightly oiled large bowl and cover with a kitchen towel or plastic wrap. Let stand in a warm place until doubled in size, about an hour.

6 Preheat the oven to 400°F. Grease a 10-inch round cake pan with oil. Once the barmbrack has risen, tip out onto a floured board again and knead it once more, then place in the pan. Cover and let stand again in a warm place until it has risen, about an hour.

7 Once risen, brush with the remaining beaten egg and bake for 40 minutes. Unmold and cool on a wire rack before serving.

The bread will keep for up to 1 week in an airtight container.

Serves 6–8

1 cup raisins
1 cup dried currants
heaping ½ cup chopped candied citrus peel
½ cup Irish breakfast tea
3²⁄₃ cups all-purpose flour, plus more for flouring and kneading
½ teaspoon ground cinnamon
½ teaspoon ground nutmeg
5½ tablespoons unsalted butter, chilled and cubed, plus more for greasing
¾ cup plus 1 tablespoon milk
2½ teaspoons active dry yeast
¹⁄₃ cup plus 1 tablespoon superfine sugar
2 large eggs, beaten
oil, for greasing

My idea of heaven is sitting on Killiney Beach
in Dublin with a basket filled with tea brack, and
a flask of tea, looking out at the Irish sea

Baked Oaty Pears

During the autumn when pears are at their height of juiciness and ripeness, I love to serve this recipe for dessert after a hearty roast. You can substitute the pears for apples if you wish, or indeed ripe peaches. You can make the filling the day before baking.

1 Preheat the oven to 400°F.

2 Prepare the pears: Peel them and cut in half lengthwise. Using a teaspoon or a melon baller, scoop out the cores. Lightly toss the pear halves in the lemon juice to prevent them from browning, then set aside.

3 Place the melted butter, maple syrup, cinnamon, and finely chopped hazelnuts in a saucepan over low heat. Stir until the mixture comes together. Add the pears to the liquid, two at a time, and toss lightly to coat. Transfer the pears to a baking pan.

4 Place the oats and golden raisins in a bowl and pour over the remaining butter and maple syrup mixture from the saucepan. Mix together well.

5 Generously fill the cavities of the pears with the oat mix and bake in the oven for 20 minutes, or until the pears are tender and the top is browned.

6 Serve with whipped cream, mascarpone, or ice cream.

Serves 4

4 ripe pears
juice of 1 lemon
7 tablespoons unsalted butter, melted, plus extra for brushing
scant $^2/_3$ cup maple syrup
1 teaspoon ground cinnamon
1 tablespoon finely chopped hazelnuts
1 heaping cup old-fashioned rolled oats
2 tablespoons golden raisins

Guinness Cake

This cake can only be described as dark and majestic. The bitterness of the Guinness is balanced by the sugar and the vanilla icing adds a fluffy lightness to balance it perfectly. I make this at my restaurant, Clodagh's Kitchen, using a locally brewed stout called O'Hara's, which is similar to Guinness. If you don't like stout, worry not–you will like this cake! The caramel and coffee flavors make this cake one of the best that I have ever made or eaten… Trust me!

1 Preheat the oven to 325°F. Line the bottom of a 12-inch round springform pan with parchment paper.

2 Make the cake: Heat the butter in a large saucepan over medium heat until melted. Stir in the Guinness, then remove from the heat and stir in the cocoa.

3 In a large mixing bowl, beat the eggs, sugar, vanilla extract, and buttermilk, and then slowly mix in the Guinness mixture.

4 Sift together the flour, baking soda, and baking powder into a separate large bowl. Using a handheld electric mixer, slowly mix the wet mixture into the dry ingredients and keep beating until it is all well combined.

5 Transfer the batter to the prepared cake pan and bake in the oven for about 45 minutes. Test to make sure the cake is cooked by inserting a toothpick into the center of the cake–if it comes out clean, the cake is cooked. Let cool in the pan, then transfer from the pan onto a wire rack.

6 While the cake is cooling, make the frosting: Using a handheld electric mixer, blend all the ingredients together until light and fluffy.

7 Place the cooled cake on a plate and generously spread the frosting on top.

The cake will keep for up to 1 week in an airtight container.

Serves 10

2¼ sticks plus 1 tablespoon unsalted butter
1¼ cups Guinness
1 cup unsweetened cocoa powder, sifted
2 large eggs
2 cups plus 2 tablespoons superfine sugar
2 teaspoons vanilla extract
¾ cup buttermilk
2½ cups all-purpose flour
2 teaspoons baking soda
1 teaspoon baking powder

For the frosting
7 tablespoons unsalted butter, softened
2½ cups sifted confectioners' sugar
1 teaspoon vanilla extract
1¼ cups cream cheese (not low-fat)

Guinness adds a wonderful richness, making this the perfect Irish cake

Caraway Seed Cake

This cake is such a classic and very understated. We always have a caraway seed cake in the house over Christmas, but it's delicious at any time of the year for picnics or stored in your cake tin as an afternoon tea staple. The cake is light and crumbly, and the caraway seeds add an anise and citrus tang. Be careful not to add more seeds than specified, as they have a powerful flavor.

1 Preheat the oven to 350°F. Grease a 9½-inch round springform cake pan with butter.

2 Place the butter and sugar in large mixing bowl and cream together until the mixture is light and fluffy. Beat in the eggs and vanilla extract.

3 Sift the flour and baking powder into the mixing bowl and stir to combine. Fold in the almond flour, milk, and caraway seed.

4 Pour the batter into the prepared pan and bake for about 50 minutes, or until well risen and golden.

5 Let the cake cool in the pan for a few moments, then run a blunt knife around the edge of the pan to free the sides of the cake. Turn the cake out and let cool completely on a wire rack.

This cake will keep for up to 1 week in an airtight container.

Serves 10

1½ sticks plus 1 tablespoon butter, softened, plus extra for greasing
¾ cup plus 1 tablespoon superfine sugar
3 large free-range eggs, beaten
1 teaspoon vanilla extract
1¾ cups all-purpose flour
½ teaspoon baking powder
½ cup almond flour
2 tablespoons milk
1 tablespoon caraway seed

Traditional Irish Christmas *Plum Pudding*

For as long as I can remember, every November my mum would make a plum pudding, long enough before Christmas to allow the flavors to strengthen. The Christmas smells would waft through the house, and myself and my brother Jim would start a chorus of carols… Happy plum pudding memories.

1 Sift the flour into a large mixing bowl and, using your fingertips, rub in the chilled butter until the mixture resembles fine bread crumbs. Mix in the sugar, spices, almonds, dried fruit, citrus peel, shredded apple, and bread crumbs and set aside.

2 In a separate bowl, beat the eggs lightly, then beat in the stout, orange zest and juice, and whiskey. Stir the liquid mixture into the dry ingredients and mix well. It is traditional in Ireland that everyone in the house stirs the mixture and makes a wish. Once the wishes have been made, cover the bowl and refrigerate overnight.

3 The following day, lightly grease a 1-quart steam bowl. Pour the batter into the bowl. Cut a circle of wax paper 1½ times the diameter of the top of the bowl. Grease, then fold a single pleat in the paper to allow room for the pudding to expand during cooking. Cover the top of the bowl with the paper and secure with string.

4 Place the bowl in a saucepan and fill with water to halfway up the side of the bowl. Cover and steam for 6 hours or longer. The longer the pudding cooks, the richer and darker it becomes. Top the pan up with boiling water as required and don't let the water boil dry.

5 To store the pudding, remove the wax paper and replace with a fresh piece. Wrap the pudding in a kitchen towel and store in a cool, dry place until required.

6 To reheat the pudding, steam for 2 hours. It is traditional in Ireland to pour the Irish whiskey over the whole pudding once it is on the table. Then the youngest member of the house sets light to the pudding using a match. Once the flames have gone out, serve with softly whipped cream.

Serves 6–8

¾ cup plus 2 tablespoons all-purpose flour
7 tablespoons butter, chilled and cubed, plus more for greasing
1 cup packed dark brown sugar
½ teaspoon freshly grated nutmeg
½ teaspoon ground cinnamon
½ teaspoon ground cloves
²/₃ cup chopped almonds
²/₃ cup each golden raisins, raisins, and dried currants
¼ cup chopped candied citrus peel
1 small baking apple, peeled, cored, and shredded
1 cup dried white bread crumbs
2 large free-range eggs
¹/₃ cup Irish stout
zest and juice of 1 orange
3 tablespoons Irish whiskey

To serve
3 tablespoons Irish whiskey
softly whipped cream

GOOD MORNING *Ireland*

Summer Berry Granola Parfait

This granola parfait is a permanent fixture on the breakfast menu at my restaurants. I change the berries depending on the season. We have such delicious yogurts in Ireland, due to our outdoor free-ranging cows fed on green pastures. It's the trio of different textures and flavors that makes this parfait such a palate pleaser. If you are serving a crowd for breakfast, you can make them up the night before and keep them in the fridge overnight.

1 In a bowl, mix the chia seeds with the yogurt.

2 Now layer the parfait ingredients in glasses to serve—yogurt first, then granola, followed by the fresh berries. If the glasses are tall enough, you can repeat the layering.

3 Decorate with a sprig of mint and serve.

Serves 4

2 teaspoons chia seeds
¾ cup plus 1 tablespoon organic plain Greek yogurt
2 cups Honeyed Coconut and Cinnamon Granola (page 49)
1¼ cups mixed fresh summer berries
sprigs of mint, to decorate

How to Make the Perfect Pot of Irish Tea

1 First, fill a teapot with hot water from the faucet to warm it up.

2 Fill the descaled kettle with fresh cold water. Just before the kettle begins to boil, drain the warm water from the teapot and add 1 teaspoon leaf tea per person to the pot, plus an additional teaspoonful "for the pot."

3 As soon as the kettle comes to a boil, pour ¾ cup boiling water per person into the teapot. Let the tea steep for about 4 minutes, depending on the desired strength.

4 Add cold milk or lemon to teacups, depending on the preference of your guests. Pour the tea into the cups, using a tea strainer to catch the loose leaves.

How to descale your kettle with a lemon
Slice 1 whole lemon and place in an empty kettle. Fill the kettle with cold water and bring to a boil. Once the kettle has boiled, drain the water and repeat the process three times using the same lemon. The result is a descaled kettle that will make the best-tasting cup of tea.

Apple, Pecan and Cinnamon *Porridge*

During the winter months, we start the day at home with a big pot of porridge. It's nutritious, warming and sets you up for the chilly day ahead. The creaminess of the porridge works beautifully with the sweet apples, cinnamon and crunchy pecans. Bananas, nutmeg, and roasted hazelnuts are also delicious additions to porridge.

1 Pour the oats and milk into a saucepan and place over medium heat. Bring to a boil, then reduce the heat and simmer for 10 minutes, stirring frequently.

2 Halfway through cooking the porridge, stir in the ground cinnamon.

3 A couple of minutes before the porridge is cooked, stir in the shredded apple. Stir in more milk (or water) if you would like the porridge thinner.

4 Once the porridge is cooked, pour into warm bowls to serve. Sprinkle the chopped pecans over the porridge and drizzle with the honey.

Serves 4

2 cups old-fashioned rolled oats
2½ cups milk, plus more if required
1 teaspoon ground cinnamon
1 apple, cored and shredded

To serve
⅓ cup finely chopped pecans
2 tablespoons golden honey

Honeyed Coconut and Cinnamon Granola

Homemade granola really is worth the effort, as the freshness and flavor are far superior to any store-bought version. There is very little preparation involved– the only thing that is time-consuming is the gathering of ingredients. The seeds, coconut, and oats bring a delicious crunchiness (plus many health benefits!) and the honey and cinnamon add much-welcomed sweetness! Sprinkle it over porridge or yogurt–or use it as the base for my delicious Summer Berry Granola Parfait (page 46).

1 First make the granola: Preheat the oven to 350°F.

2 Place the coconut oil, cinnamon, honey or syrup, and vanilla extract in a small saucepan over low heat and stir until all the ingredients are melted and combined.

3 In a large bowl, combine the oats, dried fruit, nuts, seeds, and coconut. Pour over the melted coconut oil and honey mixture and stir well until all the dry ingredients are evenly coated.

4 Tip the granola mixture onto a large baking sheet. Using the back of a wooden spoon, spread it out evenly. Bake in the oven for 20 minutes, stirring every 5 minutes so that it is evenly toasted.

5 Remove from the oven and cool, stirring every few minutes so that the granola does not stick together.

The granola will keep for up to 2 weeks in an airtight container.

Serves 4

7 tablespoons coconut oil
2 teaspoons ground cinnamon
$^2/_3$ cup golden honey or apple syrup
1 teaspoon vanilla extract
$5^1/_2$ cups old-fashioned rolled oats
2 cups mixed dried fruits, such as chopped apricots, golden raisins, or cranberries
$1^1/_4$ cups coarsely chopped hazelnuts
scant $^2/_3$ cup pumpkin seeds
$^1/_2$ cup sunflower seeds
1 cup dry unsweetened shredded coconut

Green Goddess Juice

I juice daily. It's something I started doing about two years ago when my workload accelerated, and I found I didn't have the energy that I used to have in my twenties… Ever since I started juicing, I get fewer colds and my skin and overall health have improved. This might not be for everyone, but it works for me. I admit I am now addicted! I don't use juices as a substitute for food, but rather a substitute for coffee. The spirulina, though it doesn't taste too wonderful, is packed with protein, vitamins and minerals.

1 Wash the spinach, kale, apple, cucumber, and celery, then chop.

2 In a juicer, blitz all the ingredients along with 3 tablespoons water, until smooth, adding a bit more water to loosen if necessary.

3 Garnish with a celery stalk and a sprig of mint and serve.

Makes 1

1½ cups (packed) baby spinach leaves
3 ounces kale
½ apple, quartered, cored, and chopped
¼ cucumber
¼ stalk of celery
1 mint leaf
juice of ½ lemon
¼-inch piece fresh ginger
1 teaspoon spirulina powder

To garnish
½ celery stalk
1 sprig of mint

Smashed Avocado and Knockalara Toasts

This is one of my best-loved breakfast dishes. It's the creaminess of the ripe avocado, the saltiness of the Knockalara (a feta-style cheese), and the freshness of the mint on crunchy sourdough toast that make me crave this for breakfast all the time! The Knockalara cheese I use is made in County Waterford in Ireland by Agnes and Wolfgang Schliebitz from sheep's milk and is one of my favorite Irish cheeses. I love the crumbly texture and the lemon and salt flavors. If you can't get your hands on this wonderful cheese, you could substitute it with good-quality feta.

1 In a bowl, mash the avocado using a fork. Add the mint and lemon juice and mix well.

2 Crumble in the cheese, season with sea salt and black pepper, and mash again.

3 Toast the slices of sourdough bread and smear with the smashed avocado and cheese.

Serves 2

1 ripe avocado, peeled, halved, and pitted
1 tablespoon finely chopped mint
juice of ½ lemon
3 ounces Irish Knockalara or good-quality feta cheese
sea salt and freshly ground black pepper
2 slices sourdough bread

Irish Croque Madame

We love our toasted cheese and ham sandwiches in Ireland, usually eaten for lunch at the pub, but this is a luxurious version that I started having on my trips to France and it's now a firm favorite in my house. It's the ultimate comfort food for breakfast, brunch, or indeed lunch. Oozy melted Gabriel or Gruyère cheese sauce drizzled over cooked ham, peppery mustard, and soft fried egg layered over crunchy toast… what's not to like?! If you are in a hurry, you could omit the cheese sauce and just use shredded cheese instead.

1 Start by making the cheese sauce: In a saucepan, melt the butter over low heat, then stir in the flour until a dough ball forms—this is called a roux. Increase the heat to medium and very slowly beat in the milk, a bit at a time. Keep beating until you get a thick white sauce. Next, beat in the cheese and nutmeg. Season to taste with sea salt and black pepper and set aside.

2 Make the sandwiches: Preheat the broiler to medium heat. Place the bread under the broiler and toast on one side. Remove from the broiler and smear 1 tablespoon of the cheese sauce on each slice. Place a slice of cooked ham on top, followed by a smear of Dijon mustard. Top each slice with equal amounts of shredded cheese and then close the sandwiches.

3 Place the sandwiches back underneath the broiler until the cheese has melted.

4 While the sandwiches are toasting, in a skillet, melt the butter over medium heat and crack in the eggs. Fry them, covered, until the whites are just set and the yolks are still runny, about 3 minutes.

5 Top each sandwich with a fried egg and serve immediately.

Serves 2

For the sauce
2½ tablespoons butter
¼ cup plus 1 tablespoon all-purpose flour
1 cup milk
½ cup shredded Irish Gabriel or Gruyère cheese
¼ teaspoon freshly grated nutmeg
sea salt and freshly ground black pepper

For the sandwiches
4 slices white sourdough bread
4 slices fully cooked ham
1 tablespoon Dijon mustard
1 heaping cup shredded Irish Gabriel or Gruyère cheese
1 tablespoon butter
2 large free-range eggs

Baked Eggs 5 Ways

I adore baked eggs. Given the small amount of effort that you have to put into preparing them, they make such a delicious and decadent breakfast. Just follow the main method first and then add any topping you wish.

1 Preheat the oven to 400°F.

2 Grease a small ovenproof dish with the butter and season with salt and black pepper. Crack both the eggs into the dish.

3 Add your chosen topping and bake in the oven for 10 minutes.

Serves 1

2 teaspoons butter
sea salt and freshly ground black pepper
2 large free-range eggs
toasted sourdough bread cut into strips, to serve

Toppings

Coolea Cheese and Smoked Bacon Egg
Sprinkle half a cooked smoked bacon slice, diced, on top of the eggs. In a bowl, place ¼ cup shredded aged Coolea cheese or Gruyère, ½ teaspoon Dijon mustard, and 1 tablespoon half and half. Mix well and pour over the eggs and bacon. Season and bake.

Pulled Ham Hock, Spinach, and Basil Baked Egg
Sprinkle 1 tablespoon crumbled cooked ham hock on top of the egg, followed by ⅓ cup torn baby spinach, 1 teaspoon torn basil, and 1 tablespoon half and half. Season and bake.

Full-Irish Baked Egg
Top the eggs with half a cooked breakfast pork sausage link, sliced, half a cooked blood sausage, crumbled, half a cooked bacon slice, diced, and half a cherry tomato, sliced. Pour 1 tablespoon half and half on top. Season and bake.

Smoked Salmon Baked Egg
Dice a slice of smoked salmon and place in a bowl, followed by ½ teaspoon finely chopped chives and 1 tablespoon half and half. Mix well and then pour over the eggs. Season and bake.

Spinach, Nutmeg, and Mushroom Baked Egg
Slice 1 portobello mushroom (or 2 button mushrooms) and sauté in a pat of butter, until lightly browned. Place the mushrooms on top of the eggs, followed by ⅓ cup torn baby spinach, a sprinkling of freshly grated nutmeg, and 1 tablespoon half and half. Season and bake.

Coolea Cheese Eggs Benedict with Zucchini

Coolea is one of my favorite Irish farmhouse cheeses. It is made in the beautiful mountains of West Cork. The business was started by Dick and Helene Willems in 1979, and the cheese is now made by their son Dicky and his wife Sinead. Aged Coolea is similar to a very good well-aged Gouda, and has delicious nutty, buttery, and salty flavors. You can use this Coolea cheese sauce to go alongside a roast chicken, pasta, or potato dumplings. Make sure to chargrill the zucchini on a very hot pan so that they get nice and crispy. You could substitute the zucchini with asparagus, if you like.

1 First make the cheese sauce: Melt the butter in a saucepan over medium–low heat, then stir in the flour and cook for 1 to 2 minutes. Using a wire whisk, beat in the milk to make a smooth sauce. Simmer gently for 5 minutes and season with salt and white pepper. Stir in the cheese and nutmeg, and continue stirring until the cheese has melted.

2 Meanwhile, poach the eggs: Place a saucepan of salted water over high heat. When it has come to a boil, using a spoon, give the water a good swirl. Crack your eggs into a cup (one at a time) and bring the egg in the cup (again one at a time) as close to the boiling water as possible before quickly dropping the egg into the swirling water (the swirling motion helps the white of the egg to form around the yolk). Reduce the heat to medium and cook the eggs for 3 minutes. (Another trick is to add a generous amount of vinegar to the poaching liquid. This helps the eggs form into perfect spheres, but sometimes you can taste the vinegar in the eggs, so the cupping method is what I suggest.)

3 While the eggs are poaching, place a skillet over high heat and add the olive oil. When the oil is hot, tip in the zucchini and season with salt and pepper. Cook for a couple of minutes on each side.

4 Toast the sourdough bread and arrange on 2 plates. Arrange 2 poached eggs on each piece of toast. Pour over the cheese sauce and place the zucchini on top. Season with salt and black pepper and serve.

Serves 2

4 large free-range or organic eggs
2 tablespoons olive oil
1 zucchini, sliced
sea salt and freshly ground
   black pepper
2 slices sourdough bread, to serve

For the cheese sauce
2 tablespoons butter
3½ tablespoons all-purpose flour
2½ cups milk
sea salt and white pepper
3½ ounces Coolea cheese or
   good-quality Gouda
a pinch of ground nutmeg

Smoked Salmon with Buttery Truffled Eggs

We have so many fabulous smokehouses in Ireland producing some of the
finest smoked salmon in the world… Belvelly, Burren, Woodcock and Ummera
are just some of the ones that I love. Try not to overcook the scrambled eggs,
as you want them to be loose and buttery. The shavings of fresh truffle are
the cream on the cake in this recipe, but if you can't get your hands on fresh
truffles, use grated nutmeg instead.

1 Crack the eggs into a bowl, season with salt and black pepper,
and pour in the cream. Beat until well combined.

2 In a medium-size saucepan, heat the butter over low heat. Once
the butter has melted and is foamy, stir in the scrambled egg
mixture with a wooden spoon. Cook, stirring continuously, until
the egg begins to cook but is still a bit runny. Remove from the
heat.

3 Spoon the scrambled eggs onto two warm dishes and shave a
little of the truffle on top.

4 Arrange two slices of smoked salmon on each plate beside the
truffled eggs and serve.

Serves 2

5 or 6 large free-range eggs
sea salt and freshly ground
   black pepper
3½ tablespoons half and half
5½ tablespoons butter
½ small fresh black truffle
4 slices Irish smoked salmon

Irish Breakfast *Tortilla*

When I have friends or family staying over, this is what I make them for breakfast. It's such a great, fun dish to cook when you have a lot of mouths to feed. You can prepare it before everyone rises from their beds and keep it warm in a low heat oven, then slice it like a cake.

1 First prepare the onion and potato: Peel both vegetables, cut in half, and then thinly slice. Pat them dry with a clean kitchen towel or paper towels.

2 Place a 9-inch, nonstick skillet over medium heat and pour in 1 tablespoon of the oil. When the oil is hot, tip in the onion and potato, reduce the heat, and let cook for 10 minutes, making sure you come back to the pan every few minutes to stir.

3 Meanwhile, crack the eggs into a large bowl, season with salt and pepper, and beat lightly. When the onion and potato are cooked, tip them into the bowl of beaten eggs, and mix together.

4 Place the pan back over low heat and add the remaining tablespoon of oil. Tip in the sausages and smoked bacon lardons and cook for 5 minutes. Then tip into the egg mixture.

5 Place the pan back over the heat and, if needed, add a splash more of oil. Pour in the tortilla mixture, arrange the halved cherry tomatoes on top, and cook for about 15 minutes, or until the tortilla is set.

6 Every now and then, draw the edge in gently with a spatula. After about 10 minutes, you need to turn the tortilla over to cook on the other side. Place a plate over the pan and carefully invert both so that the tortilla is on the plate. Put the pan back on the heat and tip the tortilla back in, this time the other way up.

7 Let the tortilla cook for another 2 minutes, then let rest in the pan for about 5 minutes. Slide it onto a board or plate and serve sliced, either warm or at room temperature.

Serves 2

1 onion
1 large potato (9 ounces)
2 tablespoons olive or canola oil, plus more if needed
5 large free-range eggs
sea salt and freshly ground black pepper
2 country-style pork sausage links, cut into 1-inch slices
3½ ounces smoked bacon lardons
4 cherry tomatoes. halved

Poached Eggs, Pulled Ham, and Hollandaise
on Herby Potato Cakes

A Sunday brunch dish at its best! Try not to over-poach the eggs, as the oozing yolks make this dish utterly delicious.

1 First, make the potato cakes: Cook the potatoes in a large saucepan of boiling salted water until tender, about 15 minutes. Drain, transfer to a bowl, and mash with a potato masher.

2 While the potatoes are still hot, mash in the crème fraîche or sour cream, egg yolk, and mustard. Season with salt and black pepper, then mix in the parsley. Add the flour to the potato mixture—this will help to make the consistency suitable for rolling out. Transfer the potato mixture to a floured work surface and, using a rolling pin, roll it out to a thickness of about 2 inches. Using a 4-inch cookie cutter, cut out four potato cakes. Melt the butter in a skillet and fry the potato cakes gently on both sides, until golden brown.

3 Meanwhile, make the hollandaise sauce: Melt the butter in a saucepan over medium heat. While the butter is melting, pour the egg yolks into a food processor, followed by the lemon juice. Turn the food processor to medium speed and slowly pour the melted butter in through the feed tube, until incorporated with the egg yolks and the mixture is a thick consistency.

4 Poach the eggs according to the instructions in step 2 on page 56.

5 To serve, arrange the potato cakes on two warm plates (two potato cakes per person) and divide the ham hock evenly between them, placing it on top of the cakes. Next, place one poached egg on top of each cake. Pour over the hollandaise sauce, season with sea salt and black pepper, and serve.

Serves 2

4 large free-range eggs
3½ ounces pulled ham hock
3½ tablespoons butter
sea salt and freshly ground black pepper

For the herby potato cakes
1¼ pounds potatoes, peeled and cut into small chunks
¼ cup crème fraîche or sour cream
1 large free-range egg yolk
1 teaspoon Dijon mustard
sea salt and freshly ground black pepper
2 tablespoons freshly chopped flat-leaf parsley
1 tablespoon all-purpose flour, plus more for flouring
2 tablespoons butter

For the hollandaise sauce
7 tablespoons butter
2 large free-range egg yolks
juice of 1 lemon

Cinnamon Baked Beans

I know that it may seem like an effort to make baked beans from scratch, but it is so worth it! These make a delicious addition to my Full-Irish Breakfast (page 67) or are great simply eaten as a light meal with some bacon and toast.

1 In a large saucepan, heat the olive oil over medium heat and stir in the shallots and garlic. Sauté for 3 minutes.

2 Stir in the tomatoes, tomato paste, cinnamon, brown sugar, vinegar, and 2 cups water. Bring to a boil and stir well.

3 Tip in the beans, reduce the heat to very low, and let simmer, uncovered, for 1 hour, or until the sauce is thick.

4 Season with salt and black pepper before serving.

To make these baked beans extra special, you could add any of the following to step one: 2 slices pancetta or streaky bacon, chopped; ¾ cup chopped cooked ham; or 1 cup chopped chorizo.

Serves 4

2 tablespoons olive oil
5 ounces shallots, peeled and finely chopped
2 garlic cloves, peeled and grated
1 (14½-ounce) can diced tomatoes
2 tablespoons tomato paste
1 teaspoon ground cinnamon
½ cup plus 1 tablespoon dark brown sugar
²/₃ cup red wine vinegar
1 (15-ounce) can navy beans, drained
sea salt and freshly ground black pepper

Irish Eggs *with Black Pudding*

We make these Irish-style scotch eggs in my restaurants. Served with cucumber pickle and spicy apple chutney, they are utter heaven! Black pudding is one of the best traditional foods produced in Ireland and it adds a lovely richness, but if you are not a fan, leave it out and double the quantity of sausage meat.

1 In a saucepan of cold water, bring the eggs to a boil over high heat. Reduce the heat and simmer for exactly 7 minutes. Drain and cool the eggs under cold running water, then remove the shells.

2 While the eggs are cooking, prepare the meat: Blend the blood sausage, sausage meat, thyme, parsley, mustard, lemon zest, scallion, and salt and pepper until well combined. You can do this with a wooden spoon, with your hands, or in a food processor.

3 Flour your hands and work with a quarter of the sausage mixture at a time.

4 Roll the meat into a ball. Put it on a piece of plastic wrap and press slightly.

5 Cover with another sheet of plastic wrap and gently roll out into a circle about 2 inches in diameter. Remove the top sheet of plastic wrap and place a hard-cooked egg in the center of the sausage mixture circle.

6 Close the sausage mixture around the egg, using the plastic wrap underneath as an aid, and reshape until you have the perfect egg shape. Remove all the plastic wrap. Repeat with the remaining eggs and sausage mixture.

7 Coat the Scotch eggs: Place the flour in one bowl, the beaten egg in a second bowl, and the bread crumbs in a third. Dip each Scotch egg into the flour, then the egg, then roll it in the bread crumbs.

8 Place a shallow pan over medium heat and pour in the oil until it is about two-thirds full. When the oil is hot, carefully drop in the Scotch eggs and fry them for 10 minutes, turning every few minutes to ensure they are evenly fried and golden brown. Remove from the oil and drain on paper towels. Serve at room temperature.

Makes 4

4 large eggs
canola or sunflower oil, for
   pan-frying

For the meat coating
3½ ounces blood sausage
3½ ounces sausage meat
1 teaspoon finely chopped thyme
   leaves
1 tablespoon finely chopped flat-leaf
   parsley
1 teaspoon Dijon mustard
zest of 1 lemon
1 scallion, finely chopped
sea salt and freshly ground
   black pepper

For the bread crumb coating
1 cup all-purpose flour, plus more
   for flouring
1 large egg, beaten
1 cup very fine plain dried
   bread crumbs

Homemade *Fennel and Pork* Sausages

We love sausages in Ireland, whether it be for breakfast, lunch, or dinner. These are what you might call "gourmet sausages." There are lots of variations that you can use, for example chile and ginger, puréed sundried tomatoes and olives, fresh thyme and garlic, or dried oregano and feta cheese. Delicious served with Soda Bread Farls (page 19) or Herby Potato Cakes (page 62).

1 In a skillet, lightly dry-roast the fennel seeds over medium heat for 2 minutes, tossing all the time. Remove from the heat and finely chop.

2 Place the toasted fennel in a mixing bowl along with the ground pork, garlic, bread crumbs, and egg. Season with salt and black pepper. Mix well using clean hands or a wooden spoon.

3 Divide the mixture into 10 pieces and roll each one into a sausage shape. Place them on a baking sheet lined with baking parchment, cover with plastic wrap, and chill in the refrigerator for 1 hour (this will help the sausages to hold their shape).

4 Place a large skillet over medium heat. Add the olive oil and heat for 1 minute. Then, one by one, add the sausages to the pan and cook gently for about 10 minutes, turning every couple of minutes to make sure they are evenly cooked.

For a traditional "bangers and mash," pair these homemade sausages up with any of my 5 ways of making Creamed Potatoes (page 179).

Serves 2

2 teaspoons fennel seed
1 pound ground free-range pork, neck or shoulder meat
2 garlic cloves, crushed
1¼ cups fine fresh white bread crumbs
1 large free-range egg, beaten
sea salt and freshly ground black pepper
2 tablespoons olive oil, for pan-frying

Full-Irish *Breakfast*

Oh yes, the full-Irish breakfast, the craving of every Irish person if they have been away from Ireland for too long… I grew up having this every Sunday after mass, as we had to fast before receiving Holy Communion, and so we would be starving by the time we got home. Serve this with a piece of good-quality bread fried in the pan after you have fried the eggs, so that the bread soaks up all the leftover flavors. I know it's sinful and not healthy, but it tastes so good!

1 Place a skillet over medium heat and add the butter and olive oil.

2 Once the butter has melted, add the bacon slices and pan-fry until cooked, about 3 minutes each side. Transfer to a large warm plate in a low oven to keep warm. Pan-fry the sausage in the skillet until browned on all sides and cooked through, then add to the bacon in the oven.

3 Add the blood sausage, tomatoes, and mushrooms to the skillet and sauté until browned on all sides, adding more butter to the pan if needed. Once they are all cooked, transfer to the plate in the oven.

4 Meanwhile, heat the beans in a saucepan.

5 Finally, cook the eggs. Add more butter to the skillet if needed. Crack the eggs into the pan and season with salt and black pepper. After about a minute, baste the eggs by tilting the pan, spooning up some of the melted butter and pouring it over the eggs. Continue to baste every minute and cook the eggs until they are done to your liking, 3 to 4 minutes for a firm white and a still-runny yolk.

5 To serve the breakfast, divide all the cooked ingredients among four warm plates and serve with the brown soda bread.

Serves 4

3½ tablespoons butter, plus more
 if required
1 tablespoon olive oil
8 cured bacon slices
8 Irish breakfast pork sausage links
4 slices of black blood sausage
4 slices of white blood sausage
2 medium beefsteak tomatoes,
 halved
7 ounces portobello mushrooms,
 sliced
1 (13.7-ounce) can beans with
 tomato sauce or 1 (15-ounce) can
 baked beans
4 large free-range eggs
sea salt and freshly ground
 black pepper
4 slices brown soda bread, to serve

MIDWEEK *Suppers*

Colcannon Soup with Parsley Pesto

This soup reinterprets the Irish classic "colcannon," a dish that is made of mashed potatoes and kale or cabbage. You could add some pulled pork or pancetta to this soup if you wish. Delicious served with my Cheese and Rosemary Savory Scones (page 18).

1 Melt the butter in a heavy-bottomed saucepan over medium heat. Add the potatoes, onions, garlic, and nutmeg, stir, and cover the pan with a lid. Reduce the heat to low and let sweat for about 15 minutes, stirring occasionally.

2 Add the hot stock and bring the heat up to high. Let the onions and potatoes cook in the stock until they are completely soft, then add the cabbage—it will only take 5 minutes to cook.

3 While the cabbage is cooking, in a food processor, place all the ingredients for the parsley pesto and blend until you have a smooth consistency. Set aside.

4 When the cabbage has wilted, stir in the cream, then pour the soup into a blender and blitz until smooth. Season with salt and pepper. If necessary, return to the pan to warm through.

5 To serve, pour the soup into bowls and garnish with a generous drizzle of the parsley pesto.

Serves 6

3½ tablespoons butter
10½ ounces potatoes, peeled and diced
3½ ounces onions, peeled and diced
2 garlic cloves, crushed
½ teaspoon freshly grated nutmeg
3⅓ cups hot chicken or vegetable stock
14 ounces savoy cabbage, sliced
¾ cup plus 1 tablespoon half and half
sea salt and freshly ground black pepper

For the parsley pesto
4 ounces flat-leaf parsley
scant ⅔ cup extra virgin olive oil
scant ¼ cup pine nuts, toasted
1 garlic clove, crushed
½ cup freshly grated Parmesan cheese

Smoked Bacon and Cabbage *Soup*

Bacon and cabbage—a quintessential Irish combination. The crispiness of the bacon, the sweetness of the tomatoes, the sharpness of the cabbage, and the comfort of the potatoes make for a delicious soup. Be sure to buy good-quality canned tomatoes. If you are cooking this when tomatoes are in season, you can use fresh tomatoes, finely chopped. Once you have added the cabbage, don't cover the pan, as the steam will dull its green color.

1 Place a heavy-bottomed saucepan over medium heat. Add the butter, and, when it has melted, stir in the smoked bacon, potatoes, garlic, and onions. Cover the pan with a lid and cook for 10 minutes.

2 Add the stock and tomatoes and bring to a boil. Tip in the cabbage, reduce the heat, and cook until all the vegetables are tender, about another 5 minutes. Season to taste with salt and pepper and serve with buttered chunky bread.

Serves 6

3½ tablespoons butter

3½ ounces smoked bacon, diced, or smoked bacon lardons

4½ ounces potatoes, peeled and diced

2 garlic cloves, crushed

1 onion, chopped

2 cups hot chicken or vegetable stock

1 can (14½-ounce) diced tomatoes

10½ ounces savoy cabbage, shredded

sea salt and freshly ground black pepper

Potato and Wild Garlic *Soup*

I love the subtle flavor of wild garlic. It has a rounder, softer flavor than a garlic bulb. When I lived in West Cork I would forage for wild garlic during the spring in the forests along the seashore–the perfect growing grounds for wild garlic. It has a very elegant, long, broad, green leaf with a subtle aroma. It is so delicious in this soup because potatoes are wonderful at holding other flavors. The flowers are less flavored but are so beautiful for garnish.

1 Place a heavy-bottomed saucepan over medium heat and melt the butter. Add the onion and potatoes and stir well. Cover the pan with a lid and cook for 10 minutes. Add the stock and chopped fresh garlic leaves and bring to a boil. Reduce the heat and cook until the potatoes are tender, about 10 minutes.

2 Transfer to a blender and blitz until the soup has a smooth consistency. Stir in the half and half, and warm through over a medium heat for a couple of minutes.

3 Season with salt and pepper and serve with a sprinkle of wild garlic flowers, if available, on top.

Serves 6

3½ tablespoons butter
¾ cup coarsely chopped onion
1 pound potatoes, peeled and
   roughly chopped
4 cups hot chicken or vegetable
   stock
a large handful of wild garlic leaves
⅓ cup plus 1 tablespoon half and
   half
sea salt and freshly ground
   black pepper
wild garlic flowers (if available),
   to garnish

Nettle and Wild Garlic *Soup*

Your first reaction to nettle soup is probably "Ouch!" But worry not: once nettles are cooked, they loose their sting. When foraging for nettles, search for the small, young leaves with tender stalks–and wear gloves! Nettles are similar to spinach in flavor and are also packed with iron. Nettle soup has a great history in Irish cuisine. My grandfather, who was a fisherman in Cobh County Cork, used to make it for its iron content.

1 In a medium-size saucepan over medium heat, place the butter. When the butter has melted, add the onion and potatoes. Stir, cover with a lid, and reduce the heat to low. Let sweat for about 10 minutes, stirring occasionally.

2 Pour in the hot stock and increase the heat to high. Let the onions and potatoes cook in the stock until they are completely soft.

3 Using gloves, add the nettles (they will lose their sting once cooked), wild garlic, and freshly grated nutmeg. Stir and cook until the nettles and wild garlic are wilted, 10 minutes.

4 Pour the mixture into a blender and blitz until you get a smooth consistency. Season with salt and black pepper and return to the pan.

5 Stir in the half and half and place over medium heat to warm through, 2 minutes.

6 Serve in warm bowls, garnished with wild garlic flowers.

Serves 4

3½ tablespoons butter
1 onion, peeled and diced
¾ pound potatoes, peeled and diced
3⅓ cups hot chicken or vegetable stock
3½ ounces young nettle leaves and tender stems
3½ ounces wild garlic leaves
½ teaspoon freshly grated nutmeg
sea salt and freshly ground black pepper
½ cup half and half
wild garlic flowers, to garnish

Roasted Parsnip and Apple *Soup*

The sweetness of the apple is delicious in this soup, but if you don't like the idea, just leave it out and add an extra parsnip. This is perfect as a lunch dish, but is elegant enough to serve as a starter for a dinner party or for Sunday lunch. The garnish of crispy bacon, apple and cilantro adds another level of texture and flavor to this soup, so it's worth the effort.

1 In a saucepan, melt the butter over low heat and stir in the onion, garlic, potato, parsnips, and apple. Season with salt and pepper. Cover the pan with a lid and cook until the parsnips and apple are tender, stirring occasionally, about 10 minutes.

2 Remove the lid and stir in the flour and curry powder, stirring continuously to coat all the ingredients evenly and ensuring no lumps form.

3 Pour in the hot stock, stirring well, and bring to a boil. Reduce the heat and simmer for another 10 minutes.

4 Pour the soup into a food processor and blend to a smooth consistency. Stir in the cream.

5 Pour back into the saucepan and gently warm through (the half and half will have brought the temperature of the soup down).

6 To serve, pour the soup into bowls and garnish with either julienned apple, crispy bacon lardons, or finely chopped cilantro.

Serves 4

3½ tablespoons butter
1 onion, peeled and coarsely chopped
1 garlic clove, crushed
1 potato, peeled and coarsely chopped
3 parsnips, peeled and coarsely chopped
1 baking apple, peeled, cored, and coarsely chopped
sea salt and freshly ground black pepper
1 tablespoon all-purpose flour
1 tablespoon medium curry powder
1 quart hot vegetable stock
⅓ cup plus 1 tablespoon half and half

To garnish
julienned apple, crispy bacon lardons, or fresh cilantro

Carrot, Ginger and Orange Soup *with* *Hazelnut* and *Cilantro Pesto*

I love adding orange and ginger to carrots—they add zest and zing. When you are making the hazelnut and cilantro pesto, don't blend it too fine, as the texture is nicer when it's a bit chunky. You can substitute the hazelnuts with toasted pine nuts or almonds. Drizzle a swirl of cream around the soup to garnish, and there you have the tricolor of the beautiful Irish flag.

1 In a saucepan, melt the butter over low heat and stir in the onion, garlic, potato, ginger, and carrots. Season with salt and black pepper. Cover and cook, stirring occasionally, until the carrots are tender, 10 minutes.

2 Remove the lid and pour in the hot stock. Stir well and bring to a boil, then reduce the heat and simmer for another 15 minutes. Halfway through, stir in the orange zest and juice.

3 Meanwhile, make the pesto: Place all the ingredients in a food processor and blitz for a few seconds—the pesto should be chunky and not too blended. Transfer to a bowl and set aside.

4 When the soup is cooked, transfer it to the food processor and blend to a smooth consistency. Return to the pan to warm through, if necessary.

5 To serve, pour the soup into warm bowls and garnish with the chunky hazelnut and cilantro pesto.

Serves 4

3½ tablespoons butter
1 onion, coarsely chopped
1 garlic clove, crushed
1 potato, peeled and coarsely chopped
2-inch piece fresh ginger, peeled and grated
3 carrots, peeled and coarsely chopped
sea salt and freshly ground black pepper
4¼ cups hot chicken or vegetable stock
zest and juice of 1 orange

For the hazelnut and cilantro pesto
3½ ounces fresh cilantro leaves and finely sliced stalks
1/3 cup hazelnuts, toasted
½ cup freshly grated Parmesan cheese
2/3 cup extra virgin olive oil

Irish Onion Soup with Smoked Cheese Toasties

I love onion soup, especially during the winter months. When teamed with a big smoked Gubbeen cheese crouton, it makes the ultimate bowl of comfort food. The key to this great soup is making a good-quality beef stock (see below) and making sure you caramelize the onions until they are a deep brown color.

1 Preheat the oven to 350°F.

2 In a heavy-bottomed saucepan over gentle heat, place the butter. Once melted, tip in the onions, cover, and sweat until soft, stirring once or twice, 10 minutes. Then remove the lid and stir in the garlic. Continue to cook until the onions are golden brown.

3 Pour in the white wine and cook until it has evaporated.

4 Next, add the finely chopped thyme and stock, and stir. Let simmer on gentle heat for 20 minutes. Season to taste with sea salt and black pepper.

5 Place the toasted bread circles on a baking sheet and sprinkle the shredded smoked cheese on top. Heat in the oven until the cheese has melted, 2 to 3 minutes.

6 Pour the soup into warmed bowls and place the cheese toasts on top.

Serves 4

7 tablespoons butter
10 sweet onions, peeled and thinly sliced
2 garlic cloves, peeled and crushed
½ cup white wine
1 teaspoon finely chopped thyme
1 quart hot beef stock
sea salt and freshly ground black pepper

For the croutons
4 slices toasted good-quality bread, cut into large circles
3½ ounces Smoked Gubbeen cheese (or good-quality smoked cheddar), shredded

To make a beef stock, brown 3lb marrow bones, either by roasting or frying, until the bones are brown, then add 1 chopped onion, 1 celery stalk, 2 carrots, 1 leek, and a whole bulb of garlic, and continue to brown. Then place the bones and vegetables in a saucepan, cover with 4 cups cold water, and stir in a spoonful of tomato paste, a splash of red wine, a sprig of thyme, a bay leaf, and some freshly ground black pepper. Simmer gently for 4 hours with the lid on slightly askew so that the stock can reduce and concentrate. Drain and discard the bones and vegetables—and there you have a lovely beef stock.

Smoked Haddock *Chowder*

This is the chowder recipe that I serve in my restaurants. I took it off the menu one season and there was such an uproar that I had to reprint the menus and put it back on again—yes, it's that good! Irish smoked haddock swimming in rich cream, wine, leeks, and garlic makes for a big pool of deliciousness that I would like to swim in daily! You could also add fresh mussels or cockles at the same time you add the smoked haddock, or substitute with smoked mackerel.

1 Set a saucepan over medium heat and melt the butter.

2 Stir in the onion, leek, and garlic. Reduce the heat, cover, and let sweat for 5 minutes. Remove the pan from the heat and add the wine. Return the pan to the heat and cook for another 3 to 4 minutes. Pour in the stock, milk, and potatoes and bring to a boil. Reduce the heat and simmer for 10 minutes.

3 Stir in the fish chunks and continue to cook for 5 minutes. Add the half and half and chives and season to taste with salt and pepper. Cook for another 5 minutes, then serve.

Serves 6

3½ tablespoons butter
1 onion, finely diced
1 leek, finely sliced
2 garlic cloves, crushed
⅓ cup plus 1 tablespoon dry white wine
2 cups fish stock
1¼ cups milk
10½ ounces potatoes, peeled and diced
2¼ pounds undyed smoked haddock (finnan haddie), skin removed and cut into small chunks
1 cup half and half
chives, finely sliced, to garnish
sea salt and freshly ground black pepper

Irish Lamb Stew *with Pearl Barley*

This is one of my all-time favorite comfort foods… I grew up having this exact recipe once a week, and I would imagine the same goes for most Irish people. We all have our own variations of Irish stew and, when cooked right, this dish is so delicious. Make a very well-flavored stock, use good-quality lamb, and thicken the casserole juices to make a gravy. It's a fantastic mid-week supper for the whole family. It can be made the night before and reheated.

1 First make the stock: Place all the ingredients in a saucepan with 2 quarts cold water. Bring to a boil and then simmer for as long as possible to bring out the flavor, 2 to 3 hours if you can. Strain the stock and set aside.

2 Preheat the oven to 300°F.

3 Place a casserole dish over high heat, melt the butter, and add the lamb. Season with salt and pepper and stir until it is a nice brownish color. Transfer to a plate and repeat the process with the vegetables, before also transferring them to a plate.

4 Spoon all the vegetables, the lamb, and the pearl barley into the casserole dish, placing the potatoes on top (you do not want them to get mushy). Remove all the leaves from the thyme stems (discard the stalks) and add them to the dish. Cover with the hot lamb stock and place in the oven for 1½ hours.

5 While the lamb stew is cooking, make a roux: Melt the butter in a saucepan and beat in the flour, until it forms a paste. Once the casserole has cooked, ladle the juices from the stew into a saucepan and slowly beat into the roux. Cook, stirring, until thickened and smooth. Then pour the thickened gravy back into the stew before serving.

Serves 6

2 tablespoons butter
2 pounds boneless lamb for stew, cut into chunks
sea salt and freshly ground black pepper
4 carrots, peeled and cut into 2-inch pieces
4 onions, peeled and cut into thin wedges
6 waxy potatoes, peeled and cut into 2-inch pieces
½ cup pearl barley
2 sprigs of thyme

For the stock
1 lamb bone
1 carrot
1 onion
2 peppercorns
1 bouquet garni

For the roux
2 tablespoons butter
2 tablespoons all-purpose flour

Dublin Coddle

Coddle is one of the most traditional dishes in Dublin. In the days when Catholics were not supposed to eat meat on Fridays in Ireland, this was a dish eaten on Thursdays, as it allowed families to use up any remaining sausages or bacon. I have varied the recipe to my own taste by adding cream, pancetta, and herbs, as I love the extra flavors that they bring. If you want to keep it traditional, omit these extras, but I think it tastes better with them. Pearl barley is delicious in a coddle–just stir in ½ cup pearl barley after adding the chicken stock.

1 In a casserole dish, melt the butter over medium heat and stir in the onions. Cover and let sweat for 5 minutes.

2 Remove the lid from the pan and stir in the bacon or pancetta. Cook for another 5 minutes.

3 Stir in the chopped sausage, followed by the carrots and potatoes. Cook for a couple of minutes.

4 Pour in the hot stock and cream, followed by the thyme.

5 Season with sea salt and black pepper and stir. Bring to a boil, then reduce the heat and let simmer for 25 minutes.

6 Once the coddle is cooked, stir in the flat-leaf parsley and serve.

Serves 4

3½ tablespoons butter
2 medium onions, diced
6 smoked bacon or pancetta slices, diced
1 pound Irish pork sausage links, cut into ¾-inch chunks
8 baby carrots, left whole
9 ounces potatoes, peeled and cut into ¾-inch dice
1¼ cups hot chicken or beef stock
¾ cup plus 1 tablespoon half and half
1 teaspoon finely chopped thyme
sea salt and freshly ground black pepper
1 tablespoon freshly chopped flat-leaf parsley, to serve

Comforting Chicken Broth

Somedays I just want to be comforted with a pure chicken broth that makes me feel nourished and warm... It's what I make when someone (or myself) is feeling a bit down or has a cold. You can make it on a sunny day and freeze it for a rainy day. This recipe is delicious on its own, but you could use it as a stock for risotto or soups.

1 Break up the chicken carcass into 6 to 8 pieces. Place them in a saucepan with the pearl barley, onion, carrot, celery, bay leaf, nutmeg, and peppercorns.

2 Cover the carcass and vegetables with 6½ cups cold water. Place the pan over medium heat and slowly bring to a boil, then reduce the heat to low and simmer for 2 hours.

3 Strain the liquid into a separate saucepan and add the parsley. Season the broth with salt and black pepper and reheat if necessary.

4 You can add shredded cooked chicken, or ribbons of carrot and zucchini, if you wish.

Serves 6

1 chicken carcass
¼ cup dry pearl barley
1 onion, peeled
1 carrot, peeled
1 celery stalk
1 bay leaf
¼ teaspoon freshly grated nutmeg
5 black peppercorns
2 teaspoons finely chopped
   flat-leaf parsley
sea salt and freshly ground
   black pepper

Seaweed and Vegetable Salad

This salad is permanently on the menu in my restaurants. Packed with vitamins and minerals, it is health on a plate. But it also tastes fantastic, full of fresh, zesty, sweet flavors, and crunchy textures. Sea spaghetti is a brown, spaghetti-like edible seaweed that grows in abundance on the shores of Ireland. It has more of a nutty flavor than a strong sea flavor. Sea spaghetti is very high in iron, and you can find the dried version in most health food stores—simply rehydrate it when you want to cook with it.

1 Prepare the seaweed: In a bowl, soak the seaweed in warm water for about 5 minutes. Drain and rinse briefly (if you do not rinse the seaweed, it can be a bit too salty). Drop the seaweed into a large pot of boiling water and cook until al dente, 5 minutes. Drain.

2 In a mixing bowl, combine the beet, apple, fennel, carrot, sea spaghetti, salad greens, and chickpeas. Add the orange and lime zest and juice and extra virgin olive oil. Season with sea salt and black pepper and toss well. Sprinkle the toasted pumpkin seeds on top and serve.

Serves 6

$3/4$ ounce dry Irish sea spaghetti
1 beet, peeled and grated
1 apple, peeled, cored, and grated
$1/2$ head fennel, grated
1 carrot, peeled and grated
2 cups loosely packed salad greens
$1/3$ cup drained chickpeas, rinsed
zest and juice of 1 orange
zest and juice of 1 lime
$3 1/2$ tablespoons extra virgin olive oil
sea salt and freshly ground
   black pepper
$1/3$ cup pumpkin seeds, toasted

Roasted Butternut Squash and Goat Cheese Salad *with Orange Dressing*

The caramel flavor of butternut squash, the tangy goat cheese, the sweet orange dressing, and the crunchy pumpkin seeds create a wonderful medley of taste and texture. We have so many great goat-cheese producers in Ireland: St Tola, Bluebell Falls, and Ardsallagh are just some of them. Roasted beet works beautifully in this salad, too, so if you like, you can substitute it for the butternut squash.

1 Preheat the oven to 425°F.

2 Using a large sharp knife, cut the squash in half, scoop out the seeds, and peel. Cut the squash into ¾-inch pieces and place in a large bowl. Add the olive oil, garlic cloves, and rosemary, season with sea salt and black pepper, and toss together. Place in a roasting pan and roast in the oven for 20 minutes, or until the squash is tender.

3 Heat a skillet over medium heat and dry-roast the pumpkin seeds for a few minutes, tossing every 30 seconds. This will release the aroma from the seeds. Transfer to a bowl and set aside.

4 Make the dressing: Place all the ingredients in a small bowl and beat together using a fork. Set aside.

5 Transfer the roasted squash to a large salad bowl and discard the rosemary and garlic. Add the arugula and crumble in the goat cheese. Pour the dressing over the salad and toss lightly. Sprinkle the roasted pumpkin seeds on top and serve.

Serves 4

1 butternut squash
2 tablespoons olive oil
2 garlic cloves, peeled
1 sprig of rosemary
sea salt and freshly ground
   black pepper
⅓ cup pumpkin seeds
2½ cups arugula
3½ ounces goat cheese

For the dressing
¼ cup olive oil
2 tablespoons balsamic vinegar
1 tablespoon golden honey
1 teaspoon Dijon mustard
zest and juice of 1 orange

Pint of Shrimp *and Homemade Mayonnaise*

A pint of shrimp is a traditional pub food in Ireland. I have so many great memories of enjoying a glass of the black stuff (Guinness) with a pint of fresh shrimp and listening to traditional music in pubs in the West of Ireland. The sweetness of the shrimp is so delicious with the tangy bitterness of stout, and fresh shrimp dipped in this classic homemade mayonnaise taste so good. I have recreated this in the wine bar of my own restaurant using a local stout, O'Hara's, and local shrimp from Dublin Bay.

1 Bring a large pot of water to a boil and add a good sprinkle of sea salt. Drop the shrimp into the salted boiling water and cook for 4 minutes. Once cooked, the shrimp will have changed from a gray to pink color.

2 Drain the shrimp and let cool before you place them in an ("Imperial") pint glass.

3 To make the mayo, pour the egg yolks into a medium-size bowl, followed by the mustard, a pinch of sea salt, and the white wine vinegar.

4 Measure out the vegetable oil and extra virgin olive oil. Using a wire whisk, beat into the egg yolks gradually. The mayo will begin to get thick and creamy.

5 Serve the pint of shrimp and mayonnaise alongside a pint of Guinness.

Serves 2

sea salt
18 ounces raw medium
   shell-on shrimp

For the mayonnaise
3 large free-range egg yolks
1 teaspoon Dijon mustard
1 tablespoon white wine vinegar
$1/3$ cup plus 1 tablespoon vegetable
   oil
$1/3$ cup plus 1 tablespoon extra
   virgin olive oil

Mussels Cooked with Cream, Chorizo, Garlic, and Flat-leaf Parsley

I am a little bit biased, but I do believe that the best mussels in the world are harvested in Ireland. We are an island surrounded by strong tides and clean waters that enable mussels to grow and become beautiful, sweet cushions in rugged shells… This is one of my favorite ways to cook them, as I love the way the spiciness of the chorizo contrasts with the sweet mussels. You can substitute pancetta for the chorizo, if you like.

1 Start by preparing the mussels: The shells should be tightly shut, but if not, they should promptly close if you tap them with your finger. If they do not close, they are not alive and should be discarded. Wild mussels will have a "beard," which is a clump of fibers they use to navigate and attach themselves to rocks on the seabed. Before cooking, this beard will have to be removed. To do this, give the beard a sharp tug and pull it toward the hinge of the mussel before discarding. Next, clean the mussels in cold water to remove any sand and, using a knife, carefully scrape off any barnacles.

2 Now place a large saucepan over medium heat and add the oil, followed by the crushed garlic, chorizo, and shallots. Cover and let sweat for 2 minutes.

3 Turn the heat up to high and stir in the half and half and white wine, followed by the mussels. Stir well, cover. and cook for about 4 to 5 minutes. By then the shells should have opened, which means they are cooked. Discard any mussels whose shells have not opened.

4 Finish by sprinkling the parsley over the mussels and stirring once more to bring all the flavors together. Divide the mussels between 2 bowls and pour the remaining sauce over them before serving.

Serves 2

2¼ pounds live mussels
2 tablespoons olive or canola oil
2 garlic cloves, crushed
2¼ ounces fully cooked chorizo
    sausage, diced
2 shallots, peeled and finely
    chopped
1 cup plus 1 tablespoon half
    and half
1 cup plus 1 tablespoon white wine
1 tablespoon finely chopped
    flat-leaf parsley

Crispy Topped Cheddar *Fish Pie*

Creamy fish pie with a crunchy topping is heaven! I use panko (Japanese) bread crumbs because they crisp very nicely when baked, but if you are using regular bread crumbs, I suggest that you blend them very finely and mix them with 3 tablespoons melted butter. I use haddock in my pie, but you could also use cod, ling, hake or any similar white fish local to you.

1 Preheat the oven to 350°F.

2 Start by preparing the potatoes: Place them, whole and unpeeled, in a saucepan filled halfway with water. Cover the pan and place over high heat. When the water begins to boil, drain off about half of it, leaving just enough for the potatoes to steam. When the potatoes are cooked, about 30 to 40 minutes depending on their size, drain and peel them (hold them in a kitchen towel if they are too warm to handle), then mash them with the warm milk and the butter. Season with salt and black pepper.

3 While the potatoes are cooking, poach the fish: Pour the milk into a medium-size saucepan and place over medium heat. Add the sprig of flat-leaf parsley and the halved shallot, followed by the haddock and shrimp. Season with salt and black pepper. Bring the milk to a simmer and cook for 5 minutes.

4 Using a slotted spoon, remove the fish and shrimp from the milk and discard the parsley and shallot, reserving the milk. Transfer the poached fish and shrimp to a medium-size pie dish.

5 Now make a béchamel sauce: In a small saucepan, melt the butter and stir in the flour. Keep stirring and cooking until you have a roux (smooth paste), about 1 minute. Beat in the milk that you poached the fish in, a bit at a time, and cook until you have a thick white sauce. Stir in the dill weed. Pour the sauce over the fish.

6 Next, make the crispy cheddar topping: Mix together the cheddar, Parmesan, and panko bread crumbs.

7 Spoon the mashed potatoes over the fish pie and, using the back of the spoon, smooth the surface. Sprinkle the cheese and bread crumb mixture over the top. Bake for 25 minutes, and serve.

Serves 6

1²/₃ cups milk
1 sprig of flat-leaf parsley
1 shallot, peeled and halved
1 pound skinless haddock filet, boneless and skinless
3½ ounces peeled raw shrimp
2 tablespoons butter
3½ tablespoons all-purpose flour
1 tablespoon finely chopped dill weed

For the topping
1 pound potatoes
¹/₃ cup milk, warmed
3½ tablespoons butter
sea salt and freshly ground black pepper
½ cup shredded cheddar cheese
½ cup freshly grated Parmesan cheese
1 cup panko (Japanese) bread crumbs

Creamy Fennel and Turbot Gratin

This is what I would call a "posh" fish pie. The aniseed flavor of the fennel is so good when cooked with cream and delicate fish because the flavor travels subtly throughout. You could add a sprinkle of buttered fine bread crumbs to the top, if you want a crunchy texture. Turbot works best in this dish, but you could also use other flat fishes, such as plaice or sole.

1 Preheat the oven to 350°F.

2 Grease an ovenproof serving dish with the butter and then layer the thinly sliced fennel on the bottom of the dish.

3 Lay the turbot filets on top of the fennel and season with sea salt and black pepper.

4 In a medium-size bowl, lightly beat the cream, Parmesan, and parsley. Pour the creamy cheese mixture over the fish.

5 Bake for 20 minutes. Serve with green vegetables or broccoli rabe.

Serves 4

2 tablespoons butter
2 fennel bulbs, thinly sliced
4 x 5-ounce skinless turbot fillets
sea salt and freshly ground
   black pepper
¾ cup plus 1 tablespoon half
   and half
1 cup finely grated Parmesan cheese
1 tablespoon finely chopped flat-leaf
   parsley

*My inspiration for cooking comes
from the beautiful coastline of Ireland
—it's filled with ingredients to be
foraged and fished*

Beef and Guinness Pies *with Chocolate*

You might not expect to find chocolate in a beef and Guinness pie, but it is a match made in pie heaven! The chocolate gives a silky smooth texture and deep richness to this sublime pie filling, and cuts across the bitterness of the stout. The idea of making your own puff pastry may not appeal when comfort is the order of the day, so I have made this pie with a readymade butter puff pastry. I serve these pies with Slow-Cooked Red Cabbage (page 177).

1 Place the beef in a large bowl and sprinkle with the flour. Season with salt and pepper. Toss to coat.

2 Place a heavy-bottomed saucepan or casserole dish over medium heat and pour in 1 tablespoon of the olive oil. Add half the beef and cook, stirring occasionally, until browned, about 5 minutes. Transfer to a plate. Repeat with the remaining oil and beef, and again transfer to the plate.

3 Add the shallots, carrots, celery, garlic, mushrooms, and thyme to the pan. Stir and cook for 5 minutes. Then add the browned beef to the sweated vegetables and stir. Pour in the Guinness and add beef stock or water as required to cover the ingredients. Bring to a boil and then simmer until the meat is tender, $1\frac{1}{2}$ to 2 hours.

4 Make a roux: Melt the butter in a small saucepan with a spoonful of the liquid from the cooked meat. Stir in the flour until you have a smooth paste.

5 Strain all the liquid from the meat, then return the meat to the casserole dish. Slowly beat the liquid into the roux and cook until thickened to a sauce consistency. Add the chocolate and stir to melt. Pour the sauce back over the meat and let cool.

6 Preheat the oven to 350°F. Roll out the pastry dough on a floured work surface and use it to line 4 individual pie pans. Cut out 4 x 6-inch circles from the remaining dough to make the lids. Fill each pie to the top with the meat filling, then cover each one with a dough lid. Crisscross the dough lids lightly with a sharp knife. Brush the tops with the beaten egg, then bake the pies directly on the bottom of the oven for 45 minutes, until the pastry is cooked, puffed, and golden. Unmold and serve.

Makes 4 individual pies

$1\frac{1}{2}$ pounds organic boneless beef chuck, chopped
2 tablespoons all-purpose flour, plus more for flouring
sea salt and freshly ground black pepper
2 tablespoons olive oil
6 shallots, peeled and diced
2 carrots, peeled and diced
1 celery stalk, finely chopped
2 garlic cloves, crushed
4 portobello mushrooms, sliced
1 teaspoon finely chopped thyme
$1^2/_3$ cups Guinness
beef stock or water, as required
2 ounces unsweetened chocolate, finely chopped

For the roux
$1\frac{1}{2}$ tablespoons butter
3 tablespoons all-purpose flour

For the pie cases
15 ounces puff pastry dough, thawed if frozen
1 large egg, beaten

This is akin to having a big spoonful of Ireland in your mouth! The buttery pastry combined with the rich stew is utter heaven

Shepherd's Pie *with Colcannon Topping*

This was another staple in my house when I was growing up. There are so many variations of this classic traditional dish, but I like to keep mine simple, just adding a colcannon mash on top. You could substitute the leeks with cabbage, 1 tablespoon Dijon mustard, or 3 crushed garlic cloves. You can cook the filling ahead and freeze it if you wish, then add the potato topping after you have defrosted it. If I have leftover lamb from a roast, I will use it in this pie.

1 Preheat the oven to 350°F.

2 Place a casserole dish over medium heat and add the olive oil. When the oil is hot, add the onion, garlic, and carrots, then cover, reduce the heat, and let sweat for 5 minutes.

3 Remove the lid and increase the heat to high. Add the ground lamb and cook until browned, then stir in the tomato paste, hot stock, and frozen peas. Season with salt and black pepper and simmer over low heat for 15 minutes.

4 Meanwhile, make the colcannon topping: Place the potatoes, whole and unpeeled, in a saucepan with the largest ones at the bottom, and fill the pan halfway with water. Cover the pan and place over high heat. When the water begins to boil, drain off about half of it, leaving just enough for the potatoes to steam. When the potatoes are cooked, about 30 to 40 minutes depending on their size, drain and peel (hold them in a kitchen towel if they are too hot to handle), then place in a warm bowl.

5 In a saucepan, heat the butter over low to medium heat until melted, then stir in the leek. Cover and cook for 2 to 3 minutes. Then remove the lid and stir in the milk and nutmeg. Heat until the milk has warmed through.

6 Now mash the potatoes, gradually adding the warm milk and leek mixture, and season to taste with salt and black pepper.

7 Transfer the lamb mixture to a medium-size pie dish and spoon over the colcannon topping. Brush the top with melted butter to get a crispy golden finish. Bake in the oven for 25 minutes and serve.

Serves 4

2 tablespoons olive oil
1 onion, peeled and diced
1 garlic clove, crushed
2 carrots, peeled and diced
1 pound ground lamb
1 tablespoon tomato paste
1¼ cups hot stock (lamb or beef)
1½ cups frozen peas
sea salt and freshly ground
    black pepper

For the colcannon topping
2¼ pounds Yukon Gold potatoes
3½ tablespoons butter, plus more,
    melted, for brushing
1 leek, finely chopped
⅓ cup milk
¼ teaspoon freshly grated nutmeg
sea salt and freshly ground
    black pepper

Irish Farmhouse Chicken Casserole

This is what I cook at home when I feel a bit under the weather—the food equivalent of a big Irish hug, it's hearty and warms your bones. I have eaten similar dishes in many farmhouses around Ireland. The shallots add a lovely caramel note to the casserole, but if you are using regular onions just cut them in quarters, and they will soak up all the juices. If you are buying your chicken from a butcher, ask him for a chicken carcass to make your own chicken stock (see below).

1 Place a casserole dish over medium heat and pour in the olive oil. When the oil is warm, add the chicken and bacon and cook until lightly browned. Remove from the casserole and set aside.

2 Add the garlic, shallots, parsnips, and carrots to the casserole and lightly brown. Return the chicken and bacon to the pan and stir together.

3 In a saucepan, heat the stock over medium heat while beating in the honey and mustard. Once the stock is hot, pour it over the chicken and vegetables.

4 Stir in the chopped parsley and thyme and season with salt and black pepper. Bring to a boil, then reduce the heat and simmer for 45 minutes, covered, then serve.

Serves 4

2 tablespoons olive oil
1 organic or free-range chicken, cut into 8 pieces
4 bacon slices, chopped into ¾-inch pieces
2 garlic cloves, peeled and left whole
8 shallots, peeled and left whole
2 parsnips, peeled and chopped into 2-inch pieces
2 carrots, peeled and chopped into 2-inch pieces
2½ cups chicken stock
1 tablespoon golden Irish honey
1 tablespoon Dijon mustard
2 teaspoons finely chopped flat-leaf parsley
1 teaspoon finely chopped thyme
sea salt and freshly ground black pepper

To make a chicken stock, place a chicken carcass in a large saucepan along with 1 peeled and chopped carrot, 1 onion, 1 fennel bulb, 1 celery stalk, and some herbs. Bring to a boil, then reduce the heat and simmer for 1 to 2 hours. Drain and discard the carcass and vegetables. If you have any stock left over, fill an ice cube tray with the stock and freeze, and use for making gravy, risotto, or adding flavor to sauces.

Rabbit and Cider Stew

It may come as a surprise to many of you to read that cooking rabbit was very popular in Ireland in the early to mid-90s. Ireland, with its expanse of woodlands, boglands, and inland waterways is an ideal habitat for all manner of game. Many families, including my grandparents, were brought up on inexpensive boiled rabbit and rabbit soup—a weekly staple in many homes. Nowadays in Ireland it is less popular but many chefs like myself love to cook with it using cider or wines to deepen the flavor. For me, cider is the most delicious ingredient to cook with rabbit—its dry sweetness lightens the rich flavor of the meat. This stew is delicious with my Celery Root and Hazelnut Purée (page 187).

1 Preheat the oven to 275°F.

2 Heat a skillet over medium heat and add the olive oil. Stir in the bacon and cook until golden and crisp. Transfer the bacon to a casserole dish.

3 Add the rabbit joints to the skillet and cook until golden all over, then place in the casserole dish.

4 Lastly, add the carrots, shallots, garlic, and honey to the skillet and cook until caramelized. Transfer to the casserole dish, season with salt and black pepper, and stir in the thyme and bay leaf. Pour over the cider.

5 Cover and cook in the oven for 2 hours. Serve with the Celery Root and Hazelnut Purée.

Serves 4

2 tablespoons olive oil
10½ ounces bacon, chopped
1 wild rabbit, skinned, cleaned, and jointed
12 baby carrots
8 shallots, peeled but left whole
4 garlic cloves, peeled and crushed
2 tablespoons golden honey
salt and freshly ground black pepper
1 sprig of thyme
1 bay leaf
1²/₃ cups hard apple cider

Cashel Blue, Caramelized Onion, and Thyme *Pizzas*

Cashel Blue cheese is one of my favorite Irish farmhouse cheeses. It's made in the town of Cashel, County Tipperary, by the Grubb Family. The tangy flavor of blue cheese is fantastic with the sweet caramelized onions, and the thyme gives a subtle pepper and lemon flavor. You could use feta or goat cheese instead of the blue cheese if you wish.

1 Place the fresh yeast in a small bowl. Cover with $^1/_3$ cup plus 1 tablespoon tepid water and let stand until dissolved, 5 minutes. Place the flour in a bowl and make a well in the center. Pour the dissolved yeast into the well, then add the salt and mix in the flour from the sides. Add about $^1/_3$ cup plus 1 tablespoon water and mix into a dough. Tip out onto a lightly floured work surface and knead the dough by pushing it away from you with the back of your hand, until it has a light consistency. Place the dough back in the bowl, cover with a kitchen towel, and place in a warm place until well risen, about 3 hours.

2 While the dough is rising, prepare your topping: Place a saucepan over medium heat and add the butter. When the butter has melted, add the onions. Cover and let sweat for about 10 minutes, then remove the lid, increase the heat, and add the brown sugar. Stir the sugar into the onions until they are lovely and brown, then tip into a bowl and let cool.

3 Preheat the oven to 350°F. When the dough has risen, tip out onto a floured board and roll out to make a circular pizza shape. I like my pizzas thin, so I roll it to about $^1/_4$ inch thick.

4 Brush the pizza crust with the olive oil, then spread the onions out all over the crust. Crumble the blue cheese on top and sprinkle over the thyme. Season with salt and pepper, then bake in the oven for 20 minutes.

5 Sprinkle the arugula over the pizza just before you serve.

Makes 1 pizza (serves 2)

For the dough
2 teaspoons (scant $^1/_4$ ounce) fresh yeast
$^3/_4$ cup plus 1 tablespoon all-purpose flour, plus more for flouring
a pinch of salt

For the topping
$3^1/_2$ tablespoons butter
2 onions, quartered and thinly sliced
1 teaspoon light brown sugar
3 tablespoons olive oil
5 ounces Irish Cashel Blue cheese, or other strong blue cheese
2 teaspoons finely chopped thyme
sea salt and freshly ground black pepper
a handful of arugula

AN IRISH
Dinner Party

Cocktails

There is something so decadent about stirring up a pre-dinner or party cocktail at home. Setting up a mini cocktail bar is easy, yet looks fabulous. My advice would be to stick to one or two cocktail offerings. Set up a small table with your best glassware, an ice bucket, a cocktail shaker, stirrers, napkins, and all the required ingredients. If it's a large party, handwrite a recipe card for the cocktails so that people can mix their own—it's great fun.

Old Fashioned

Place the sugar in a glass and stir in the Angostura bitters and a splash of water. Mix well, making sure to crush the sugar. Next, add some crushed ice, along with the Irish whiskey, cherries, and orange slice. Mix well and serve.

Serves 1

½ teaspoon granulated sugar
3 dashes Angostura bitters
crushed ice
¼ cup plus 1 teaspoon Irish whiskey
2 maraschino cherries
1 orange slice

Whiskey Mojito

Reserve 1 lime wedge to garnish, and place the others in a sturdy glass with the mint and sugar. Mash together so that all of the juices of the lime and mint are released. Add some crushed ice, the whiskey, and soda water to taste. Mix well and garnish with the reserved lime wedge and a sprig of mint.

Serves 1

½ lime, sliced into thin wedges
2 sprigs of fresh mint, plus extra
   to garnish
1 teaspoon granulated sugar
crushed ice
¼ cup plus 1 teaspoon Irish whiskey
splash of soda water, to taste

Honey and Ginger

Place the lemon slice and juice in a sturdy glass, followed by the honey and ginger, and mash so that all of the juices from the lemon and ginger are released. Add some crushed ice, the whiskey, and soda water to taste. Mix well.

Serves 1

1 lemon slice
juice of ½ lemon
1 teaspoon golden honey
3 slices fresh ginger
crushed ice
¼ cup plus 1 teaspoon Irish whiskey
splash of soda water, to taste

Campari Whiskey

Place some crushed ice in a glass. In a shaker or pitcher, mix the whiskey, Campari, and vermouth together, and then pour over the crushed ice. Add soda water to taste and garnish with a twist of orange peel.

Serves 1
crushed ice
¼ cup plus 1 teaspoon Irish whiskey
4 teaspoons Campari
4 teaspoons sweet vermouth
splash of soda water, to taste
orange peel, to garnish

Wild Mushroom and Irish Ricotta *Bruschetta*

During the autumn months, an abundance of wild mushrooms grow in Ireland, and many people, including myself, forage for them in nearby County Wicklow. We are also lucky to have fresh buffalo ricotta now being produced in County Cork by Toonsbridge Dairy. The earthy flavors of the mushrooms, the creamy richness of the ricotta, and the peppery arugula leaves on crunchy sourdough bread make such a great combination. If I have more than four guests for dinner, I usually serve the mushrooms, ricotta, and arugula in individual bowls and the sourdough stacked on a wooden board, and place it all in the middle of the table for guests to help themselves… You can substitute ripe roasted vine tomatoes, grilled asparagus, or zucchini for the mushrooms.

1 Using a soft brush, clean any grit off the mushrooms, then chop them up coarsely. Place a large skillet over medium heat. Add the butter and olive oil and heat until the butter is melted. Toss in the mushrooms and garlic, season with sea salt and black pepper, then add the lemon juice. Turn up the heat and cook for 3 minutes.

2 Sprinkle the flat-leaf parsley over the mushrooms and continue to cook for another minute.

3 Meanwhile, toast the sourdough bread. Place the toast on plates and rub the halved garlic lightly over the bread to give it a subtle garlic flavor. Drizzle over 1 tablespoon of the oil, then scatter a few arugula leaves on top of the toast.

4 Pile the mushrooms on top of the arugula, dividing the juices among the plates. Using a spoon, place small dollops of the ricotta on top, then drizzle with olive oil and add a twist of black pepper.

Serves 2

For the mushrooms
3²/₃ cups wild mushrooms (such as chanterelles, morels, or ceps)
2½ tablespoons butter
2 tablespoons extra virgin olive oil
1 garlic clove, peeled and crushed
sea salt and freshly ground black pepper
juice of 1 lemon
1 tablespoon finely chopped flat-leaf parsley

For the bruschetta
2 slices sourdough bread
1 garlic clove, halved
extra virgin olive oil, for drizzling
1 cup tightly packed arugula
¼ cup ricotta cheese

Blue Cheese and *Caramelized Pear* Bruschetta

This is such a tasty and delicious starter. You can cook the pears the day before and just reheat them the next day. There are so many wonderful blue cheeses in Ireland: Cashel Blue, Bellingham Blue and Crozier Blue are some of my favorites. You can substitute apples for the pears, and hazelnuts for the walnuts, if you wish.

1 Start by preparing the pears: Peel, quarter, and core the pears, then slice them into thin wedges.

2 Place a skillet over medium heat and add the butter and honey. Stir until they are melted together. Add the pear slices to the pan and coat with the melted butter and honey. Reduce the heat and cook until caramelized, turning frequently.

3 Meanwhile, toast the sourdough bread, then brush the toast with the olive oil and rub with the garlic clove. Spread each sourdough toast with the blue cheese.

4 Transfer the toast to a warm plate and spoon the caramelized pears on top. Season with salt and pepper and sprinkle with the chopped walnuts.

Serves 4

2 ripe pears
2 tablespoons butter
2 tablespoons golden honey
4 slices sourdough bread
1 tablespoon extra virgin olive oil
1 garlic clove, peeled
5 ounces semisoft blue cheese
sea salt and freshly ground
    black pepper
a handful of walnuts, coarsely
    chopped, to serve

Artichoke and Knockalara Cheese *Soufflé*

This is such an elegant starter. The earthy flavor of the artichoke is delicious with the lemon, hazelnuts, and creamy, salty flavor of the Knockalara cheese. You could use a good-quality feta or goat cheese in this recipe, or substitute almonds for the hazelnuts. I sometimes use china cups instead of ramekin dishes as they are ovenproof and look so pretty.

1 Preheat the oven to 400°F, and place a baking sheet on the top oven rack (this will help the soufflés rise).

2 In a saucepan, cover the artichokes with cold water and add the lemon juice. Bring to a boil and then simmer until soft, about 40 minutes. Drain, transfer to a food processor, and blend to a purée.

3 Place 4 x 10 fl. oz ramekins in the refrigerator to chill.

4 In the cleaned food processor, grind the hazelnuts until finely ground. Melt half the butter and brush it over the insides of the ramekins. Sprinkle the ground hazelnuts into each ramekin and move the ramekins around so that the insides are completely coated with ground hazelnuts. Return the ramekins to the refrigerator until you are ready to fill them.

5 Next make the béchamel sauce: In a saucepan, melt the remaining butter and stir in the flour. Cook for 1 minute, then gradually beat in the milk and cook, stirring, until the sauce thickens.

6 In a large bowl, combine the puréed Jerusalem artichokes, egg yolks, thyme, and cheese, and season with salt and pepper. Stir in the béchamel sauce and then let cool.

7 Place the egg whites in a large clean bowl and, using a handheld electric mixer, beat until stiff. Using a large spoon, fold the egg whites into the artichoke mixture—do not overmix.

8 Fill the chilled ramekins with the soufflé mixture, until they are about three-quarters full.

9 Remove the baking sheet from the oven (wear oven mitts as the sheet will be hot!). Place the filled ramekins on the baking sheet and immediately return to the oven. Bake for 15 minutes and serve.

Makes 4 soufflés

10½ ounces Jerusalem
  artichokes, peeled
juice of 1 lemon
¼ cup whole skinned hazelnuts
3½ tablespoons butter
3½ tablespoons all-purpose flour
1 cup milk
3 large eggs, separated
2 teaspoons finely chopped thyme
3½ ounces Irish Knockalara cheese
  or a good-quality feta cheese,
  crumbled
sea salt and freshly ground
  black pepper

Beet Carpaccio with Arugula, Knockalara, Radishes, and Pink Grapefruit

This is such an elegant light appetizer, perfect before fish, as it is so fresh in flavor. You can cook the beets in boiling water if you prefer. I'd suggest that you use plastic or latex gloves when handling the cooked beet, as the color is hard to wash off your hands. But it is so worth it, as the sweetness of the fresh beet alongside the tangy grapefruit, peppery radish, and creamy Knockalara is a taste sensation. You could also use feta or goat cheese.

1 Preheat the oven to 350°F.

2 Roast the beets on a baking sheet for about 35 minutes, or until cooked through. You can test if they are cooked by using a teaspoon to push back the skin. If the skin comes off easily, the beets are cooked. Once ready, let them cool.

3 In a medium-size bowl, zest the grapefruit, cut away the peel, and then cut the sections of flesh into the bowl. Squeeze in the juice. Add the oil, balsamic vinegar, and radish to the bowl, and gently toss together.

4 Thinly slice the beets using a mandolin or a very sharp knife. Place the sliced beets on a serving dish.

5 Add the arugula to the bowl with the grapefruit and radish and toss together.

6 Place the arugula, grapefruit, and radish on top of the beets, then spoon the creamy cheese on top in small dollops. Season with salt and black pepper.

Serves 4

2 large beets (or 4 small), washed and patted dry
1 pink grapefruit
2 tablespoons extra virgin olive oil
1 tablespoon balsamic vinegar
4 radishes, thinly sliced
7 ounces arugula
3½ ounces Irish Knockalara cheese (or good-quality feta cheese)
sea salt and freshly ground black pepper

Smoked Mackerel and Dillisk Pâté with Fennel Crispbreads

There are so many great producers in Ireland that smoke mackerel traditionally by suspending the fish in smokehouses over slowly smoldering shavings of oak, beech, or other woods. The fish are then left overnight to be naturally infused with the smoke. I love blending dillisk seaweed through smoked mackerel as it adds a sharp flavor of the sea.

1 First, make the pâté: Place all of the ingredients in a food processor and blitz together until you get a smooth consistency. Transfer to ramekins or a large pot, cover with plastic wrap, and refrigerate for 1 hour.

2 Meanwhile, prepare the cripsbreads: Preheat the oven to 350°F and line a baking sheet with parchment paper.

3 Pour ½ cup warm water into a bowl, sprinkle in the yeast, and mix well. Let stand until the yeast foams, about 5 minutes.

4 Sift the flour into a large bowl and make a well in the center. Pour in two-thirds of the yeast mixture, then add the olive oil and a sprinkle of sea salt. Stir together until a dough forms, adding more of the yeast mixture if needed. The dough should be moist but not sticky.

5 Tip the dough onto a floured work surface and knead for 10 minutes. Transfer to an oiled bowl, cover with a kitchen towel or plastic wrap, and place in a warm, dry spot for 1 hour.

6 Divide the dough into 8 pieces and roll each piece into a rectangle about 9½ x 4 inches on a lightly floured work surface.

7 Working in batches, transfer to the lined baking sheet, brush with olive oil, and sprinkle with the fennel seeds. Push the seeds gently into the dough with the tips of your fingers.

8 Bake in the oven for 15 minutes, or until crisp and golden. Let cool on a wire rack before serving with the pâté.

Serves 8

For the pâté
14 ounces smoked mackerel filets, skinned and flaked
¾ cup plus 1 tablespoon crème fraîche or sour cream
1 tablespoon finely chopped dry dillisk (or dulse–Irish seaweed), optional
2-inch piece fresh horseradish, peeled
juice of 1 lemon
freshly ground black pepper

For the crispbreads
½ teaspoon active dry yeast
1⅔ cups all-purpose flour, plus more for flouring
2 tablespoons olive oil, plus more for oiling and brushing
sea salt
2 tablespoons fennel seeds

Crabcakes with *Tarragon Mayonnaise*

Crispy on the outside with fresh, delicate, crumbling crabmeat inside, these crabcakes are such a great taste of the Irish coast. I don't use potatoes in my crabcakes, as I think they detract from the subtle flavor of the crab. The homemade tarragon mayonnaise takes about 5 minutes to make and will keep in the fridge for a week, so make it ahead if you can. You can use fresh dill weed or basil instead of the tarragon if you wish.

1 In a bowl, place all the ingredients, except the olive oil, and season with salt and black pepper. Mix well and form the crab mixture into eight round patties. Cover with plastic wrap and refrigerate until firm, at least 1 hour.

2 When you are ready to cook, place a skillet over medium heat. Add the olive oil and heat for 1 minute. Then add the crab cakes, in batches if necessary, and cook for 3 minutes on one side. Turn them over and cook for 2 minutes on the other side. They should be golden in color. Serve with the Tarragon Mayonnaise.

Serves 4 (2 cakes each)

14 ounces lump crabmeat
4 slices stale white bread, blitzed in
 a food processor into coarse bread
 crumbs
¼ cup Tarragon Mayonnaise (see
 recipe below), plus more to serve
2 drops Worcestershire sauce
1 tablespoon finely chopped dill
zest and juice of 1 lemon
sea salt and freshly ground
 black pepper
2 tablespoons olive oil

Tarragon Mayonnaise

1 In a bowl, place the egg yolks, followed by the mustard and white wine vinegar.

2 Using a wire whisk, gradually beat in the olive oil and vegetable oil, until thick and creamy.

3 Stir in the tarragon and season with salt and pepper. The mayonnaise will keep in the refrigerator for up to 1 week.

Makes 1 scant cup

3 large free-range egg yolks
1 teaspoon Dijon mustard
1 tablespoon white wine vinegar
⅓ cup plus 1 tablespoon extra
 virgin olive oil
⅓ cup plus 1 tablespoon vegetable
 oil
1 tablespoon finely chopped fresh
 tarragon
sea salt and freshly ground
 black pepper

Fresh Oysters

My favorite way to eat very fresh oysters is straight down the hatch! When an oyster is really good, you want nothing to disturb that sublime experience, except for maybe a glass of Champagne! Saying that, a simple vinaigrette, like the one below, is very good with fresh oysters, along with sidekicks such as Tabasco sauce, cayenne pepper, lemon, wasabi sauce, celery salt and paprika. First of all, you need to know how to open an oyster…

1 On a solid worktop, place the oyster on the towel, deep shell down and hinge toward you. Cover your hand with the folded towel and hold the oyster firmly.

2 Place the tip of the knife into the crevice at the hinge, and push it in firmly. When you feel that the knife has penetrated the hinge, give the knife a twist to separate the shells.

3 Now change the position of the hand holding the oyster and, keeping the blade close to the top flat shell, slide it along to cut the muscle holding the two shells together.

4 Then run the knife underneath the oyster to sever the muscle from the deep shell. Finally, flip the oyster over in the shell, but be careful not to spill any of the delicious juices.

You will need

oysters, an oyster knife and a
  kitchen towel

Red Wine Vinaigrette

1 In a bowl, beat all the ingredients together with a fork or a small wire whisk. Pour into a small serving bowl.

2 Arrange the oysters on a large serving plate, preferably over ice, and place the vinaigrette in the center with a teaspoon to serve it with.

Makes enough for a dozen oysters

2 shallots, peeled and finely
  chopped
6 tablespoons red wine vinegar
4 teaspoons granulated sugar
salt and freshly ground black pepper
ice, to serve (optional)

Gravlax with Dill and Juniper Berries

Gravlax is such a beautiful dish. It may sound complex, but in fact it's so simple to prepare. I served this at a pop-up dinner that I held in the Whitney Museum in New York for St. Patrick's Day. I was lucky enough to find an artisan Poitín that was made in Brooklyn, so I added 2 tablespoons of that to the cure—you could also add whiskey, if you wish. I love the clean melt-in-the-mouth texture and flavor of this gravlax, so I have left out alcohol. You could substitute honey for the sugar in the cure, which gives a richer flavor.

1 First make the cure: Using a mortar and pestle (or a food processor), grind together the sea salt, sugar, juniper berries, and white peppercorns.

2 Next, lie the salmon filets, skin side down, on a sheet of plastic wrap. Spread a thick layer of dill weed on the flesh side of each filet, then add a thick layer of the dry cure, pressing it on very well.

3 Turn over one filet, skin side up, on top of the other, and wrap the plastic wrap tightly around the salmon. Place on a plate and chill in the refrigerator for 48 hours.

4 Make the dressing: In a small bowl, place the lemon juice, Dijon mustard, and extra virgin olive oil and beat together well.

5 When ready to serve, remove the cured salmon from the plastic wrap. Transfer to a large dish and drizzle with the dressing. Slice thinly.

Serves 8 (16 slices)

2 center-cut, skin-on salmon filets
(about 1 pound each)
2 tablespoons finely chopped
dill

For the cure
1 cup sea salt
¾ cup sugar
2 teaspoons juniper berries
2 tablespoons cracked white
peppercorns

For the dressing
4 tablespoons lemon juice
1 teaspoon Dijon mustard
2 tablespoons extra virgin olive oil

Salted Cod *Croquettes*

As children growing up in Cork City, we would run through the famous
English Market pinching our noses to avoid the smells of food (kids those
days!), and gasp at the long, board-like salted cods hanging from the
fishmongers' stalls. I now pass through this very same market with eyes and
nose wide open to take in all the wonderful history of food that still lies there…
For me, croquettes are so decadent and make a fun, retro starter. Serve with my
Tarragon Mayonnaise (page 119).

1 The day before you want to make the croquettes, prepare the
salted cod: In a large bowl, place the salt cod and cover with cold
water, then refrigerate for 24 hours. Drain and replace the water
twice during this time.

2 The following day, drain off the water and place the salted cod in
a large saucepan. Cover with the milk and add the sprigs of parsley.
Bring to a boil and then simmer for 30 minutes. Drain and, using a
fork, flake the fish into a bowl.

3 Place the potatoes in a saucepan and fill halfway with water. Place
over high heat and bring to a boil, then simmer until the potatoes
are cooked, about 15 minutes. Drain, add the butter, and mash well
with a potato masher.

4 In a large bowl, mix together the cooked salted cod, mashed
potatoes, crushed garlic, and chopped parsley, and season with salt
and black pepper.

5 Using a tablespoon, scoop up spoonfuls of the mixture and
form 12 cork-like shapes. Lay them on a baking sheet lined with
parchment paper. Using a pastry brush, brush the croquettes with
the beaten eggs.

6 Sprinkle the bread crumbs on a large plate and, one by one,
gently roll the croquettes in the crumbs.

7 Heat a 1-inch depth of vegetable oil in a deep skillet until
very hot and cook the croquettes until golden, turning once.
Alternatively, bake in a preheated oven at 400°F for 15 minutes.

Serves 4

14 ounces salted cod, rinsed
¾ cup plus 1 tablespoon milk
2 sprigs of flat-leaf parsley
14 ounces potatoes, peeled and
   chopped into 2-inch pieces
3½ tablespoons butter
4 garlic cloves, peeled and crushed
1 tablespoon freshly chopped
   flat-leaf parsley
sea salt and freshly ground
   black pepper
2 large free-range eggs, beaten
1¾ cups fine dried white bread
   crumbs
vegetable oil, for pan-frying

Potted Dingle *Crab*

When I serve this dish at my restaurant, I source the fresh crab from a man called Ted Browne in Dingle, County Kerry. The crab arrives in Dublin fresh twice a week, and its freshness is the reason this dish tastes so good. Ted buys the crab from local fishermen that gather the crab from local waters. It's sweet and delicate, the way crab should be. When crab is this good, it just needs complementing flavors like horseradish (for peppery tones), chile (for a little kick), and tarragon (for sweetness). Serve with Melba toast, or sourdough toast cut into strips. It's the perfect starter to any Irish dinner party and can be made a day in advance.

1 Gently squeeze out any excess moisture from the crabmeat.

2 Mix all the ingredients together and divide into 6 individual ramekins. Season with salt and black pepper.

3 Cover with plastic wrap, then place in the refrigerator and let set for 1 hour before serving. Serve with the Celery Root Remoulade, below.

Serves 6

12 ounces fresh crabmeat, picked
1 tablespoon crème fraîche
1 teaspoon hot cream horseradish
pinch of cayenne pepper, to taste
1 red chile, deseeded and
    finely sliced
6 tarragon leaves, thinly sliced
zest and juice of 1 lemon
sea salt and freshly ground
    black pepper

Celery Root Remoulade

1 Place the celery root and apple in a large bowl with the lemon juice and toss to coat. Stir in the mayonnaise, crème fraîche, mustard and parsley, and season to taste.

2 Serve 1 dessertspoon of remoulade on top of each portion of potted crab.

Serves 6

¼ head celeriac, peeled and
    sliced into matchsticks
1 red apple, quartered, cored and
    sliced into matchsticks
juice of ½ lemon
1 tablespoon mayonnaise
1 teaspoon Dijon mustard
3½ tablespoons crème fraîche
1 sprig fresh flat-leaf parsley, chopped
sea salt and freshly ground
    black pepper

Carpaccio of Irish Beef with Aged Coolea Cheese

Irish beef is so ridiculously good, especially when it has been dry-aged. I love to prepare it carpaccio-style, as you can taste the delicate pasture flavors. Carpaccio seems like a complex method, but I promise you it is actually the simplest and fastest way to prepare beef. You just need to get the best Irish beef that you can. The radishes add a lovely, peppery bite, and the aged Coolea brings a silky elegance to the plate. If you are unable to get Coolea cheese, use a well-aged Gouda instead.

1 Wrap the beef tightly in plastic wrap and freeze for 30 minutes (this will make it easier to thinly slice).

2 Make the dressing: Place the egg yolks in a small bowl and add the mustard and lemon juice, plus a little salt. Using a small wire whisk, blend together, pouring in the olive oil slowly as you beat to make a thin emulsion.

3 Thinly slice the radishes and, using a vegetable peeler, shave thin slices of the aged cheese.

4 Unwrap the beef. Using a sharp knife, slice it very thinly. Place the slices of beef between sheets of plastic wrap and flatten them out with a rolling pin.

5 Arrange 4 or 5 slices of beef on each serving plate and drizzle the dressing over the beef. Sprinkle the arugula leaves, thinly sliced radishes, and cheese on top of the beef.

6 Season well with salt and black pepper and serve.

Serves 4

7 ounces beef tenderloin steak (filet mignon)
4 radishes, trimmed
3 ounces aged Irish Coolea cheese or aged Gouda
4 cups (3 ounces) arugula leaves
sea salt and freshly ground black pepper

For the dressing
2 large egg yolks
½ teaspoon English mustard
juice of 1 lemon
⅓ cup extra virgin olive oil

Warm Beef Salad with Cashel Blue Cheese *and Walnuts*

Blue cheese, crisp romaine lettuce, crunchy walnuts, and tender, warm strips of beef, all wrapped together with a mustard balsamic dressing... there's so much flavor here! Remove the beef from the fridge an hour before you cook so that it will be at room temperature. This will make it as tender as possible.

1 Remove the steaks from the refrigerator an hour before cooking so that they come up to room temperature.

2 Place a skillet over high heat and heat for at least 1 minute. Brush both sides of the steaks with the olive oil and season with salt and black pepper. Cook them in the hot pan for 3 minutes on each side and then let rest off the heat but still in the pan for 3 minutes. This will cook them medium–rare.

3 Meanwhile, make the dressing: In a bowl, beat together the extra virgin olive oil, balsamic vinegar, Dijon mustard, and crushed garlic until a creamy dressing forms. Place the lettuce in a salad bowl and pour over the dressing. Toss well and divide the dressed salad greens among four plates

4 Slice the steaks on the diagonal, against the grain, into slices about ½ inch thick or thinner. Arrange the sliced steaks on top of the salad.

5 Sprinkle the crumbled blue cheese and chopped walnuts on top.

Serves 4

4 beef rib-eye steaks (about 5 ounces each)
2 tablespoons olive oil
sea salt and freshly ground black pepper
3½ ounces romaine lettuce
1½ cups crumbled Irish Cashel Blue or other blue cheese
⅔ cup coarsely chopped walnuts

For the dressing
4 tablespoons extra virgin olive oil
2 tablespoons balsamic vinegar
½ teaspoon Dijon mustard
1 garlic clove, crushed

Wild Mushroom and Chicken Liver Pâté

I started making chicken liver pâté about 14 years ago to sell at my stall at the farmers' markets in County Cork. Even though I now have restaurants instead of a stall, I continue my tradition of serving and selling my pâté, as I adore it. Folding wild mushrooms through the pâté adds an abundance of texture and flavor. You could also try adding caramelized onions or pancetta instead of the wild mushrooms. This is a great starter served along with some chutney or pickles and toasted brioche.

1 In a skillet, melt 3 tablespoons of the butter and add the chicken livers. Cook on medium heat, stirring occasionally, until the livers are cooked and there is no trace of pinkness, about 15 minutes. Season with salt and black pepper.

2 Transfer the cooked livers to a food processor. Add the brandy, garlic, and thyme to the skillet and deglaze all of the juices from the livers (this is where the real flavor is!). Add the brandy mixture to the food processor and blend with the livers. Let cool.

3 While the livers are cooling, cook the wild mushrooms: Place a skillet over medium heat and add the olive oil. After 1 minute, stir in the mushrooms and season with salt and black pepper. Cook the mushrooms for about 5 minutes, stirring to ensure that they cook evenly. Remove from the pan and finely chop, then let cool.

4 When everything has cooled, slowly add the remaining butter to the food processor and process until it has been incorporated, then fold in the chopped mushrooms. Transfer to a large dish or eight individual ramekins and refrigerate until set, about 3 hours. The pâté is delicious served with warm, crunchy, white bread or traditional Irish soda bread.

Serves 6

3 sticks butter
1 pound organic chicken livers, cleaned
sea salt and freshly ground black pepper
2 tablespoons brandy
2 garlic cloves, peeled and crushed
2½ teaspoons finely chopped thyme
2 tablespoons olive oil
7 ounces wild mushrooms (such as chanterelles, morels or ceps)

Beet, Blood Orange, Irish Goat Cheese, and Hazelnut Salad

This salad is so pretty, as well as being very easy on the palate, full of fresh, zesty flavors, and crunchy textures. Blood oranges are so tangy and bring such juiciness to this dish, but if you can't get hold of them, regular oranges or pink grapefruit could also be used. The goat cheese could be substituted with feta for a saltier flavor, if you like. Make double the quantity of the orange dressing, as it's a real winner over any salad.

1 Preheat the oven to 400°F. Place the hazelnuts on a baking sheet and roast for 10 minutes. Remove from the oven and chop coarsely.

2 Make the dressing: In a bowl, place all the ingredients and beat together.

3 In a salad bowl, combine the fennel, orange, beet, and salad greens, pour over the dressing, and toss lightly. Sprinkle the cheese and roasted hazelnuts on top and serve.

Serves 2

½ cup whole skinned hazelnuts
½ fennel bulb, quartered and thinly sliced
1 blood orange, peeled and segmented
3½ ounces cooked peeled beet, quartered and sliced into thin wedges
4 ounces mixed salad greens
3½ ounces Irish or other goat cheese, crumbled

For the orange dressing
½ tablespoon sherry vinegar
1 tablespoon orange juice
1 teaspoon Dijon mustard
1 teaspoon golden honey
¼ cup extra virgin olive oil

Wild Nettle Gnocchi with Cashel Blue Sauce

I call gnocchi "Irish dumplings," since they are made up of potato and flour—two ingredients that we make very well in Ireland! Velvety dumplings cushioned with earthy nettles and smothered in creamy, sweet Cashel Blue sauce and a lovely kick from the cayenne. Nettles are free and can be foraged so easily (with a pair of gloves on!), but if you aren't as charmed as I am by the nettle, you could use spinach, fresh basil, or wild garlic leaves instead.

1 Make the gnocchi: In a large saucepan, cook the potatoes, whole and unpeeled, in a small amount of boiling water until tender, about 30 minutes. Drain and let cool enough to handle. Then peel and mash them well, or put through a potato ricer into a bowl.

2 Wearing gloves to protect your hands, in a large pan of boiling water, blanch the nettles for 2 minutes. Drain and pat dry (the sting is removed once the nettles are blanched). Finely chop the nettles and fold them into the mashed potatoes.

3 Mix the egg yolks and flour into the potato and nettle mixture, and season with sea salt and black pepper. Tip the dough onto a lightly floured work surface and knead lightly until well combined. Shape into three or four balls.

4 Dust the work surface with more flour if necessary. Using your fingertips, roll one of the dough balls into a sausage about ¾ inch in diameter. Cut the dough into 1-inch pieces—these are your gnocchi. Roll the gnocchi against the front of a fork to create ridges. (This will help hold the sauce on the gnocchi once cooked.) Repeat with the remaining dough balls.

5 Make the sauce: In a saucepan, combine all of the ingredients and simmer for 10 minutes.

6 Meanwhile, bring a large pot of salted water to a boil, add the gnocchi, and cook until they have risen to the surface of the water.

7 Tip the gnocchi into a skillet, add the sauce, and gently mix together. Transfer to serving plates and serve.

Serves 4

For the gnocchi
4½ pounds russet potatoes
1 pound young nettle tips
4 large egg yolks
1¾ cups plus 2½ tablespoons all-purpose flour, plus more for flouring
sea salt and freshly ground black pepper

For the sauce
1 cup heavy cream
1 cup chicken stock
¾ cup crumbled Irish Cashel Blue cheese, or other strong blue cheese
juice of 1 lemon
¼ teaspoon cayenne pepper
sea salt and freshly ground black pepper

Dublin Bay Risotto

A few years back I spent three years living (and eating) in Italy and ever since I have had an ongoing love affair with risotto. Pairing my love of risotto with my equal love of Dublin Bay prawns makes this quite a dish! The prawns, or shrimp, are the hero of the dish. I live in Monkstown, County Dublin, which looks out over Dublin Bay, where they catch the best prawns in the world… But wherever you are in the world, buy your shrimp as fresh and locally caught as you can.

1 In a large pot, cook the prawns or shrimp in boiling salted water for 3 to 5 minutes, depending on the size, then drain and, when cool enough to handle, shell by twisting the head to remove it and pulling the legs off. Hold the tail and then lift the shell upward and away from the body. Don't throw out the shells–instead, use them to make a delicious stock by placing the shells back in the water with the other stock ingredients. Bring to a boil and let simmer for 30 minutes, then pour through a strainer. You will need 4 cups of stock for this recipe.

2 Now make a start on the risotto: In a saucepan over medium heat, melt the butter, then add the shallots or onion and garlic and cook gently until softened, 2 to 3 minutes. Stir in the risotto rice, season with salt and black pepper, and stir until the grains are coated in the butter and lightly toasted, 2 to 3 minutes.

3 Increase the heat and pour in the white wine. Let bubble for a few minutes to let the alcohol evaporate, stirring continuously.

4 Add the hot stock a ladleful at a time, cooking until absorbed before adding the next and stirring well between each addition, until all the stock has been absorbed. This will take about 15 minutes in total. After 10 minutes of cooking, stir in the peas, and a minute or two later, stir in the cooked prawns or shrimp and warm through. Just before serving, gently fold in the chopped parsley.

Serves 4

1 pound raw Dublin Bay prawns or large shell-on shrimp
4½ tablespoons butter
2 shallots or 1 small onion, peeled and finely diced
1 garlic clove, peeled and crushed
2 cups risotto rice
sea salt and freshly ground black pepper
²/3 cup dry white wine
1½ cups frozen (or fresh) peas
1 tablespoon freshly chopped flat-leaf parsley

For the stock
cooking water from prawns or shrimp
1 celery stalk, chopped
1 shallot, peeled and chopped
1 carrot, sliced
1 tablespoon tomato paste
1 bay leaf

Tomato and Fresh Irish Buffalo Mozzarella Risotto *with Desmond Cheese Crispbreads*

This dish has everything: the sweetness of the tomatoes and basil, the creaminess of the rice, the saltiness of the Parmesan, plus delicious buffalo mozzarella produced right here in Ireland.

1 Start by making the Desmond cheese crispbreads: Preheat the oven to 350°F and line a baking sheet with parchment paper.

2 Pour 1 cup warm water into a bowl and sprinkle in the yeast. Beat well. Let the yeast foam, which should take about 5 minutes.

3 Sift the flour into a large bowl and make a well in the center. Pour two-thirds of the yeast mixture into the well and add the olive oil and a sprinkle of sea salt. Stir together until a dough forms, adding more yeast mixture if needed. The dough should be moist but not sticky. Tip the dough onto a floured surface and knead for 10 minutes. Transfer to an oiled bowl, cover with a kitchen towel or plastic wrap, and place in a warm, dry spot place for an hour.

4 Divide the dough into 8 pieces and, on a lightly floured work surface, roll each piece to about 9½ x 4 inches. Transfer to the lined baking sheet. Brush with the olive oil and sprinkle with the rosemary, Desmond cheese, and pine nuts. Repeat with the remaining dough. Bake in the oven for 15 minutes, or until crisp and golden. Let cool on wire racks.

5 Next, make the risotto: In a medium-size saucepan, heat the olive oil over medium heat, add the shallots and garlic, cover, and simmer until they are translucent, about 2 minutes.

6 Stir in the rice and cook until the rice is dry, about 1 minute. Then pour in the white wine and cook until the rice has absorbed almost all of it. Add the tomatoes, season, and let the liquid come up to a bubble, then reduce the heat and simmer for a couple of minutes.

7 Add one-third of the hot stock, and, once it has been absorbed, add more stock and repeat until the rice is cooked. After about 10 minutes, gently stir in the mozzarella, Parmesan and basil. Once the rice is cooked, divide between warmed bowls and serve with the cheesy crispbreads.

Serves 4

2 teaspoons olive oil
2 shallots, peeled and very finely chopped
2 garlic cloves, peeled and crushed
1½ cups risotto rice
⅓ cup plus 1 tablespoon dry white wine
1 (14- or 15-ounce) can very good-quality crushed or cherry tomatoes
sea salt and freshly ground black pepper
2 cups hot vegetable stock
2½ cups fresh buffalo mozzerella, torn in bite-size pieces
1½ cups grated Parmesan cheese
10 large basil leaves, torn

For the crispbreads
½ teaspoon active dry yeast
1⅔ cups all-purpose flour, plus more for flouring
2 tablespoons olive oil, plus more for oiling and brushing
sea salt
1 tablespoon finely chopped rosemary
½ cup grated Desmond cheese
2½ tablespoons pine nuts, finely chopped

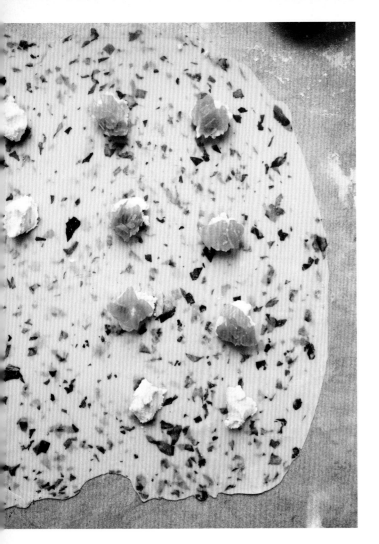

Fresh Dillisk Pasta

Ireland has an abundance of fantastic seaweed and over the past ten years it has started to make its way back onto menus across the country. Dillisk, also known as dulce, is a red alga that holds a subtle flavor of the sea and marries well with fresh pasta. This delicious fresh pasta is perfect for making the Dillisk Ravioli of Irish Smoked Salmon and Goat Cheese with Watercress Pesto on page 140.

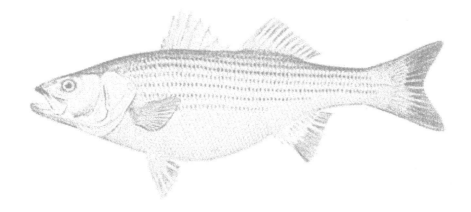

1 In a food processor, place the flour, dillisk, salt, and eggs and blend the ingredients until a dough forms. Place the dough on a floured board and knead until smooth. Divide the dough into 6 balls, cover with a kitchen towel, and let rest in a cool place or in the fridge for 30 minutes.

2 If you have a pasta machine, set it up and push the dough through the rollers 8 times. With each pass through the rollers, reduce the setting, until you reach the final setting. Be careful that your pasta does not break, as you should now have a long, thin sheet. If you do not have a pasta machine, using a rolling pin, roll the dough out very thinly. (This can be hard because it breaks easily—I would highly recommend buying a pasta machine, as they are inexpensive and so useful.)

3 Flour the pasta lightly with semolina flour and hang over a clean clothes drying rack or something similar for 10 minutes. Store in the refrigerator, wrapped in plastic wrap, and eat within 2 days.

Use this to make the ravioli on page 140, or cut into strips to make tagliatelle.

Makes about 2¼ pounds

4 cups durum flour
4 tablespoons finely chopped dry dillisk (or dulse—Irish seaweed)
a large pinch of salt
7 large eggs
semolina flour, for flouring

Dillisk Ravioli of Irish Smoked Salmon and Goat Cheese with Watercress Pesto

The smoky flavors of the salmon, the creaminess of the goat cheese and the peppery pesto make a delicious combination, and using my delicious Fresh Dillisk Pasta to create the ravioli takes this dish to the next level. You can substitute flat-leaf parsley for the watercress, if you prefer.

1 Cut the dillisk pasta sheet into strips about 4 inches wide and place teaspoonfuls of goat cheese at 3-inch intervals down the strip. Season the smoked salmon with salt and pepper and place a teaspoon of it on top of each dollop of cheese.

2 Fold the pasta over the filling and press down around it to seal it in. Cut out the pasta pillows with a sharp knife and crimp the edges with a fork to ensure that the filling does not ooze out during cooking.

3 Place a large pot of salted water over high heat and bring to a boil. Drop in the ravioli and cook for 5 minutes.

4 While the pasta is cooking, make the watercress pesto: In a food processor, place the watercress, olive oil, toasted pine nuts, garlic, and grated Parmesan and blend for a couple of minutes.

5 Drain the ravioli and return to the pot. Pour the watercress pesto on top and toss gently. Season with black pepper, and serve.

Serves 6

1 quantity Fresh Dillisk Pasta
  (page 139)
5 ounces soft goat cheese
5 ounces smoked salmon, cut
  into pieces
sea salt and freshly ground
  black pepper

For the watercress pesto
4 ounces watercress
2/3 cup extra virgin olive oil
scant 1/4 cup pine nuts, toasted
2 garlic cloves, peeled
1/2 cup freshly grated Parmesan

Lobster with Dill Gnocchi, Sea Beans and Brown Butter

Some of the best seafood that I have tasted was fresh lobster from Waterford. The clean waters and high tides in Ireland mean we have the sweetest and most tender lobsters. This is one of my favorite recipes in the book.

1 Make the gnocchi: In a large saucepan, cook the potatoes, whole and unpeeled, in a small amount of water until tender. Drain and let cool enough to handle. Then peel and mash them well. Fold the dill weed into the mashed potatoes.

2 Mix the egg yolks and flour into the potatoes and season to taste. Tip the dough onto a lightly floured work surface and knead lightly until well combined. Shape into three or four balls.

3 Dust the work surface with more flour if necessary. Using your fingertips, roll one of the dough balls into a sausage about ¾ inch in diameter. Cut the dough into 1-inch pieces–these are your gnocchi. Roll the gnocchi against the front of a fork to create ridges. (This will help hold the sauce on the gnocchi once cooked.) Repeat with the remaining dough balls.

4 Brown the butter: In a saucepan, melt the butter over medium to low heat and cook until the butter has turned brown and smells quite nutty, 5 minutes. Set aside.

5 Meanwhile, bring a large pot of salted water to a boil, add the gnocchi, and cook until they have risen to the surface of the water. Drain quickly.

6 Remove all the meat from the lobster shells, including the claws, and coarsely chop. Place a skillet over medium heat and add the olive oil, then the lobster meat. Season with salt and black pepper and add the lemon juice. Cook for 3 minutes, tossing every 30 seconds. Tip the gnocchi into the skillet and pour the brown butter over the top. Toss to combine.

7 Meanwhile, drop the sea beans into a pot of boiling water for 2 minutes, then drain. Divide the gnocchi and lobster among four warm plates with the sea beans on top.

Serves 4

5½ tablespoons butter
2 cooked lobsters
sea salt and freshly ground
    black pepper
1 tablespoon olive oil
juice of 1 lemon
7 ounces sea beans (marsh samphire
    or salicornia)

For the dill gnocchi
4½ pounds russet potatoes
3½ ounces dill, finely chopped
4 large free-range egg yolks
1¾ cups plus 3 tablespoons
    all-purpose flour, plus more for
    flouring
2 teaspoons sea salt
freshly ground black pepper

Crispy Chicken with a Creamy Irish Whiskey and Wild Mushroom Sauce

We serve this dish in my restaurants in Dublin, Clodagh's Kitchen, during the cold winter months, and it's akin to a big, warm hug in your tummy! The sweet sharpness of the Irish whiskey cuts through the cream and earthy wild mushrooms. Serve with any variation of my creamed potatoes on page 179.

1 Preheat the oven to 350°F.

2 Place an ovenproof skillet or grill pan over medium heat and add the olive oil and butter. Once they have warmed and the butter has melted, add the garlic cloves and place the chicken filets, skin side down, in the pan. Season with salt and black pepper.

3 Cook until the skin is crisp, 2 minutes, then turn over and cook on the other side for 2 minutes. Transfer the pan to the oven and cook for 20 minutes. The whole garlic cloves will add a very slight flavor to the chicken.

4 While the chicken is cooking, make the sauce: In a saucepan over medium heat, melt the butter, then add the shallots and wild mushrooms and cook for 3 minutes, stirring continuously. Pour in the whiskey and turn up the heat. Let simmer until the whiskey has reduced by half.

5 Stir in the half and half and tarragon. Season with salt and black pepper, reduce the heat to low, and cook for another 5 minutes.

6 Serve the dish on four warm plates. Divide your chosen creamed potatoes between the plates. Arrange the crispy chicken on top and spoon over the Irish whiskey and wild mushroom sauce.

Serves 4

2 tablespoons olive oil
1½ tablespoons butter
2 garlic cloves, peeled and left whole
4 supreme chicken filets (breast with wing bone attached), skin on
sea salt and freshly ground black pepper
creamed potatoes (see page 179), to serve

For the sauce
3½ tablespoons butter
2 shallots, peeled and finely chopped
10½ ounces wild mushrooms
⅓ cup plus 1 tablespoon Irish Whiskey
1¼ cups half and half
1 tablespoon finely chopped tarragon

Summer Lamb with Fennel and Roasted Nectarines

The aniseed flavor of fennel and the sweetness of rosemary work really well with lamb cutlets, but you could use this marinade for a whole leg of roast lamb. Sweet, roasted nectarines are a great companion to any lamb dish. I coat my nectarines (or peaches) with apple syrup, but you could use a good-quality maple syrup instead. These nectarines could also be served as a dessert with mascarpone or softly whipped cream.

1 Preheat the oven to 350°F and line a baking sheet with aluminum foil.

2 In a skillet, dry-roast the fennel seeds over medium heat for 30 seconds, then finely chop. Place in a large bowl, along with the rosemary, olive oil, and red wine vinegar. Season to taste with sea salt and black pepper.

3 Add the lamb cutlets to the bowl and toss to coat, then let marinate at room temperature for 10 minutes.

4 Prepare the nectarines: In a small saucepan, melt the butter and syrup together over low heat and stir. Place the nectarines on the foil-lined sheet and drizzle with the syrup mixture. Bake in the oven for 15 minutes, or until tender.

5 Heat a large grill pan over medium–high heat. Grill the lamb cutlets, turning once, until charred and cooked through, 8 to 10 minutes. Set aside to rest for 5 minutes. Just before serving, scatter with extra rosemary.

6 Make the herb salad: In a large bowl, combine the salad greens. In a small bowl, beat together the extra virgin olive oil, balsamic vinegar, and mustard to combine. Season to taste with sea salt and black pepper, drizzle over the salad, and toss to coat. Serve with the lamb and sweet nectarines.

Serves 4

For the lamb
1 teaspoon fennel seeds
½ sprig of rosemary, finely chopped, plus more to serve
2 tablespoons olive oil
1 tablespoon red wine vinegar
sea salt and freshly ground black pepper
4 thick lamb cutlets (about 3½ ounces each)

For the nectarines
3 tablespoons butter
⅓ cup plus 1 tablespoon High Bank Orchard syrup or good-quality maple syrup
2 nectarines, halved and pitted

For the salad
1 head baby romaine lettuce, leaves separated and coarsely torn
1½ cups loosely packed mixed salad greens
2 tablespoons extra virgin olive oil
2 teaspoons balsamic vinegar
½ teaspoon Dijon mustard

Venison, Chile, and Chocolate Stew

This dark, velvety stew is irresistible. The chocolate adds a smooth, dry, smoky, and slightly bitter flavor, but is quickly sweetened by the parsnips and red wine. I love using venison in stews as the meat gets so tender and is so full of flavor. We are lucky to be able to have wild vension in Ireland–our cuisine is so rich in wild game that I would need a separate book to cover it. If you are not a fan of venison, you could substitute it with pork or beef. But I urge you to give venison a go in this stew–you'll love it. You could serve this with my Garden Herbed Hasselback Potatoes (page 182)

1 Preheat the oven to 300°F.

2 Place a casserole dish over medium heat and add the olive oil. Add the bacon or pancetta and cook for 3 minutes, stirring continuously. Then stir in the shallots, garlic, and parsnips and cook until caramelized. Remove everything from the casserole and set aside.

3 Place the flour in a bowl and add the venison. Toss to coat, then shake off any excess flour and add the venison to the casserole over high heat. Sprinkle over the smoked paprika. Cook until the venison is browned on all sides, then remove from the casserole and set aside.

4 Keep the casserole on the heat and deglaze by adding the red wine and stirring all the juices into the wine. Cook until reduced to two-thirds of its original volume, then return the bacon or pancetta, shallots, garlic, parsnips, and venison to the pot.

5 Pour in the stock, followed by the chocolate and whole chile, and bring to a simmer. Season with salt and black pepper, stir, and then cover the casserole with a lid. Cook in the oven for 1 to 1½ hours, until the venison is very tender. Remove the whole chile before serving.

Serves 4

2 tablespoons olive oil
½ cup diced smoked bacon or pancetta
5 ounces shallots, peeled and left whole
4 garlic cloves, peeled and crushed
4 parsnips, peeled and chopped into 1-inch pieces
2 tablespoons all-purpose flour
1 pound diced boneless venison
1 tablespoon smoked paprika
1 cup red wine
3 cups beef stock
2 tablespoons shredded semisweet chocolate or dark chocolate nibs
1 whole red chile
sea salt and freshly ground black pepper

Slow Cooked Pork Cheeks, Vermouth, and Gooseberries with Celery Root Purée

Pork and gooseberries are such a wonderful combination. Even if it's just a simple pork chop or roast pork loin that you are cooking, a gooseberry sauce will bring it to heightened tastebud delights! Pork cheeks have recently become popular in Ireland, as they are cheap to buy and full of flavor once they are paired with the right ingredients. They do taste a lot better when slow-cooked, as they become tender and succulent. The vermouth cuts through the fat of the pork, adding a sweet flavor, but you could use white wine instead if you wish. The celeriac purée is delicious served alongside these pork cheeks.

1 Preheat the oven to 275°F.

2 Prepare the pork cheeks: Trim the excess fat around the edges, but leave some fat on the cheeks, as that adds great flavor.

3 Place a casserole dish over high heat and add the olive oil. Once the oil is warm, seal the pork cheeks on each side, then pour in the stock and vermouth. Add the sprigs of thyme and the gooseberries. Season with salt and black pepper.

4 Cover the casserole dish and place in the oven for 2 hours.

5 While the pork cheeks are slow-cooking, make the celery root purée: Place the celery root in a saucepan and cover with cold water. Then place over high heat and bring to a boil. Once the water has started boiling, reduce the heat and simmer until the celery root is cooked through, about 15 minutes. Drain and set aside.

6 In a small saucepan, combine the butter, half and half, and nutmeg and gently warm over low heat, then pour over the cooked celery root. Season and mash well or beat with a wire whisk.

7 To serve, spoon the celery root purée onto four warm plates and place the cooked pork cheeks on top. Spoon the gooseberries and sauce from the casserole dish over the pork cheeks.

Serves 4

8 pork cheeks
2 tablespoons olive oil
1²/₃ cups chicken stock
³/₄ cup plus 1 tablespoon dry
    vermouth
2 sprigs of thyme
7 ounces gooseberries
sea salt and freshly ground
    black pepper

For the celery root purée
1½ pounds celery root (celeriac),
    peeled and cut into chunks
3½ ounces butter
¹/₃ cup plus 1 tablespoon half
    and half
¼ teaspoon freshly grated nutmeg
sea salt and freshly ground
    black pepper

Irish Farmhouse
Cheese Board

In Ireland, we have spectacularly good artisan cheesemakers, so a simple cheeseboard can make the best ending to a dinner party. I prefer to serve oatcakes or water crackers with my cheese board, as they don't detract from the cheese flavor so much. It's lovely to serve fresh fruits such as grapes, sliced pears, and apples to cleanse the palate between cheeses, and I also serve chutneys such as my Apple and Raisin Chutney (page 224), or quince jelly, fig jam, or Irish honey with the cheese

When I am putting together a cheese board, I usually choose about three or four cheeses, but sometimes, when I come across a superb, perfectly ripe cheese, I will just serve that on its own. So, try some of the great Irish farmhouse cheeses and I guarantee you'll discover something fabulous! My suggestions for an Irish cheese board would be:

Hard

Desmond–cow's cheese with a hard, quick impact, and a sharp resonant aftertaste.
Aged Coolea–Gouda-style cow's cheese with a deep, intense flavor, and toffee notes.
Corleggy–raw goat cheese with a smooth and salty, piquant flavor.

Semi-hard

Durrus–raw cow's milk cheese with a washed rind and a sweet, fragrant, nutty flavor.
Gubbeen–cow's milk cheese with a washed rind and buttery, hazelnut flavors.
Ardrahan–cow's milk cheese with a washed rind and a creamy, salt, and hazelnut flavor.

Soft

Cooleeney–Camembert-style soft cow's cheese with a distinct mushroomy aroma and a rich, semi-liquid interior.
Carrigbyrne–very soft and creamy cow's cheese, with notes of salted butter and mushrooms.

Fresh

St Tola–raw organic goat cheese with fresh, creamy, and sweet flavors.
Bluebell Falls–goat cheese with a smooth, creamy texture; very fresh on the palate.
Knockalara–a creamy, fresh, crumbly, feta-style sheep's cheese.

Blue

Crozier Blue–rich, creamy, blue sheep's milk cheese.
Cashel Blue–creamy, mild, blue cow's milk cheese, slightly granular in texture.
Bellingham Blue–raw milk, creamy blue cheese, robust and rich in flavor.

SUNDAY *Lunch*

Poached Whole Salmon *with Pistachio Yogurt*

My grandfather was a fisherman in Cobh, County Cork, and had one of the first wild salmon fishing licences in the county, so fresh wild salmon was a big part of my life from an early age. The season for wild salmon fishing is a very short one in Ireland, running from June to August, and when I get my hands on my first wild salmon of the year, I get so excited about being lucky enough to cook and eat this precious king of the sea. I like to poach my salmon whole, as this method is the most delicate way of cooking the fish, and the meat just crumbles off the bone. If you don't have a fish kettle, you could cut the salmon into three parts and poach in a saucepan. I love the tanginess and freshness of the Pistachio Yogurt but you could also serve it with my Cucumber Pickle (see page 227).

1 Place the whole salmon in a fish kettle and cover with cold water, making sure that the water covers all of the fish. Add the bay leaves, sprigs of fennel, lemon, and peppercorns, and season with sea salt. Bring to a boil, then turn off the heat and let the salmon cool completely in the water.

2 Once cooled, drain off the water and let the salmon drain free of any water. Using a paring knife or your fingers, carefully remove the skin from the salmon.

3 Prepare the salmon: Transfer the fish to a large serving plate. Very thinly slice the cucumber (using a mandolin if you have one) and place the thin slices along the center of the length of the fish. Garnish the rim of the salmon with the sprigs of fennel and lemon wedges.

4 Make the pistachio yogurt: In a bowl, mix together the yogurt, lime zest, and finely ground pistachios.

5 Serve the salmon with the pistachio yogurt on the side.

Serves 10

For the salmon
1 whole salmon (about 5½ pounds), cleaned and scaled
3 bay leaves
3 sprigs of fennel
1 lemon, cut into wedges
1 teaspoon black peppercorns
sea salt

To garnish the salmon
½ cucumber
5 sprigs of fennel
1 lemon, cut into thin wedges

For the pistachio yogurt
1²/₃ cups plain Greek yogurt
zest of 2 limes
1 tablespoon pistachios, finely ground (I use a mortar and pestle)

Tarragon and Mustard Chicken with Potato Stuffing

Tarragon and mustard are a beautiful combination. One big tip that I will give you is that when you are marinating the chicken, it is important to rub the flavored butter under the skin of the chicken before roasting it, as the flavors will penetrate right into the meat. We love stuffing in Ireland and my potato stuffing is a winner—with flavors of celery, garlic, and thyme, it's a classic with roast chicken. You may think it's a bit odd that I place the turnips under the chicken, but the flavors of the turnip will penetrate through.

1 Preheat the oven to 400°F.

2 Place the softened butter in a bowl and stir in the mustard and finely chopped tarragon. Season with sea salt and black pepper and mix well. Rub three-quarters of the tarragon and mustard butter all over the chicken and between the skin and the breast meat.

3 In a small saucepan, melt the remaining tarragon and mustard butter over medium heat. Place the baby turnips in a bowl and pour the melted butter on top. Toss to coat.

4 Make the potato stuffing: In a saucepan, melt the butter over medium heat. Stir in the onions, celery, and garlic, cover, and sweat for 2 minutes. Then remove the lid and stir in the potato, thyme, and bread crumbs. Season with sea salt and black pepper and cook for 5 minutes, stirring often so that it does not burn. Remove from the heat and let cool before stuffing the chicken.

5 Stuff the chicken with the potato stuffing, making sure the cavity is only two-thirds full. This will allow hot air to circulate inside the cavity so that the chicken will cook properly.

6 Put the buttered turnips in a roasting pan along with the sprigs of tarragon and place the whole chicken on top. Transfer to the preheated oven and roast for 1 hour 20 minutes, or until the juices run clear when the thickest part of the thigh is pierced with the tip of a knife. Baste the chicken halfway through cooking.

7 Once the chicken has cooked, remove from the oven and cover with aluminum foil. Let rest for 15 minutes and then carve.

Serves 4

1¾ sticks butter, softened
1 tablespoon Dijon mustard
3 tablespoons finely chopped
  tarragon, plus 3 sprigs
sea salt and freshly ground
  black pepper
1 whole (about 3½ pounds) chicken
8 baby turnips

For the potato stuffing
2½ tablespoons butter
5 ounces onions, peeled and
  finely diced
1 celery stalk, finely diced
1 garlic clove, peeled and crushed
1¼ pounds potatoes, peeled
  and diced
1 teaspoon finely chopped thyme
2 cups fine stale bread crumbs

A Traditional Irish Christmas Turkey
with Sausage, Herb, and Apple Stuffing

My childhood memories of Christmas lunch start on Christmas Eve. The turkey was the focal point of activity. This enormous bird would sit on the kitchen table being fussed over, dressed, stuffed, seasoned, and surrounded by tiny sausages. My parents would take it in turns to get up in the night to baste it and adjust the temperature. By Christmas morning, the whole house was infused with the aromas of sage, bacon, and turkey smells. We all had our favorite bits—dark meat or white, leg or breast, and for me, crispy skin was a real treat. I do love the tradition of the big bird and all the trimmings. It's not just the ingredients, it's the passing on of family tradition. Every one has their own stuffing recipe with that secret ingredient that makes all the difference; their own way of making the perfect roast potatoes and diehard rules about when to take the turkey out of the oven and how to make the gravy. So here's wishing you a deliciously good old-fashioned Irish Christmas.

1 Preheat the oven to 450°F.

2 If you are using a frozen turkey, it's best to thaw the bird in the refrigerator. A turkey will need about 24 hours to thaw for every 4 to 5 pounds. If your turkey is fresh, it is best to store it in the refrigerator if at all possible. Take the turkey out of the refrigerator 1 hour before roasting to let the meat relax and come to room temperature, which will make it more tender.

3 Remove the giblets from inside the bird's cavity—these cannot be cooked with the turkey. Keep them for when you are making turkey stock or gravy. Wash the cavity and wipe with paper towels—make sure it is completely dry.

4 Carefully separate the turkey's skin from the flesh, trying to avoid breaking the skin. Place 3 or 4 bacon slices under the skin of each breast—this will let the flavor of the bacon run directly into the turkey meat and also keep the meat moist. Wrap several bacon slices around each leg, interlacing them to keep them in place. Lay bacon slices across the top of the whole bird, crisscrossing them.

Serves 8

1 free-range or organic turkey
(about 8½ to 10 pounds)
16 bacon (or pancetta) slices

For the stuffing
3½ tablespoons butter
1 onion, finely chopped
1 apple, cored and chopped into
¾-inch pieces
8 ounces pork sausage meat
2 cups fresh white bread crumbs
2 teaspoons finely chopped thyme
1 tablespoon finely chopped flat-leaf
parsley
¼ teaspoon freshly grated nutmeg
sea salt and freshly ground
black pepper

5 Next, make the stuffing: In a saucepan, melt the butter in a saucepan over medium heat. Stir in the onion and apple, then cover and sweat for 2 minutes. Remove from the pan and let cool.

6 Place the cooled onion and apple in a large mixing bowl and stir in the sausage meat, bread crumbs, thyme, parsley, and nutmeg, and season with salt and black pepper. Mix well, making sure all the ingredients are evenly distributed throughout the sausage meat.

7 Fill the cavity of the turkey two-thirds full with the stuffing. It should only be two-thirds full to let air circulate on the top of the cavity so that the turkey can cook. The stuffing has much more flavor when cooked in the cavity, but if you prefer not to do so, you can place it in an ovenproof dish and cook it in a preheated oven at 350°F for 25 minutes.

8 Line the roasting pan with the shallots, carrots, parsnips, garlic, and thyme, and place the stuffed turkey on top.

9 Place the pan in the oven and immediately reduce the heat to 350°F. After 45 minutes, take the turkey out and baste the drippings from the pan over the turkey. Cover loosely with aluminum foil and return to the oven for another 3¼ hours (that's 4 hours in total)–check the cooking timetable (see right) to match the weight of your turkey. Continue to baste the turkey every 45 minutes.

10 Check to see if the turkey is cooked by inserting the tip of a sharp knife into the thickest part of the thigh; the juices should run clear. When you have taken the turkey out of the oven, let rest for 30 minutes with a loose tent of foil over the top to keep it warm. This lets the juices redistribute themselves, giving tastier meat.

For the roasting pan

4 shallots, peeled and halved

3 carrots, peeled and cut into 3-inch pieces

3 parsnips, peeled and cut into 3-inch pieces

1 whole garlic bulb, halved horizontally through the center

4 sprigs of thyme

Turkey cooking times

7¾ to 11 pounds
3 hours 20 minutes to 4 hours 40 minutes

12 to 14¼ pounds
4 hours 40 minutes to 5 hours 20 minutes

14¼ to 17½ pounds
5 hours 20 minutes to 6 hours 40 minutes

17½ to 19½ pounds
6 hours 40 minutes to 7 hours 20 minutes

17½ to 19½ pounds
7 hours 20 minutes to 8 hours 40 minutes

Cork Spiced Beef

It was a tradition when I was growing up that my dad would buy spiced beef from the English Market in Cork City every Christmas to be cooked for our family supper on Christmas Eve. We would all bundle into the house in the late afternoon after all the Christmas shopping rush was over to be welcomed with the smell of these delicious spices wafting from the kitchen. We would usually serve up a whole cooked ham alongside the spiced beef. Because the beef has been marinated for such a long period, once it comes to the cooking stage it is already incredibly tender, and once cooked it just crumbles in your mouth. The saltpeter can be hard to find; the best place to get it is online or in a specialist food store. There isn't really an alternative to using saltpeter–its function is to preserve the red color of the meat. This spiced beef is delicious served with my Beet and Horseradish Cream (page 177).

1 First prepare the beef: Trim the meat of any excess fat.

2 Rub the sugar well into the beef, then place in a bowl, cover with plastic wrap, and refrigerate for 12 hours.

3 The following day, using a mortar and pestle, grind together the spices, saltpeter, and salt. Rub the spice and salt mix over the meat, re-cover, and refrigerate for 6 to 7 days, turning daily.

4 Transfer the beef to a large, heavy-bottomed saucepan, add the turnip, and cover with cold water. Bring to a boil and then let simmer for 2 hours. Lift out into a serving dish and let cool. Serve cold.

Serves 10

1 beef boneless rump or top sirloin roast (about 6½ pounds)
⅓ cup firmly packed dark brown sugar
3½ tablespoons allspice berries
2½ tablespoons black peppercorns
3½ tablespoons juniper berries
1 teaspoon grated nutmeg
2½ tablespoons cloves
1 tablespoon saltpeter
⅓ cup sea salt
1 turnip, peeled and coarsely chopped

Crispy Ginger Pork Belly with Red Cabbage and Apple Slaw

Pork belly is one of my favorite cuts of meat to cook with, because there is so much flavor in it–plus the crispy skin is worth all the effort of being the cook, as you can sneak a piece before you bring it to the table! Ginger, honey, chile pepper, and lemongrass are a burst of fabulous flavors that the pork belly revels in. The red cabbage and apple slaw is even better if you make it a few hours before you serve so all the flavors settle into each other. And the best part is, they are both fabulous together the day after your roast in a sandwich!

1 Either ask your butcher to score the skin of the pork belly at ½-inch intervals, or do it yourself using a very sharp knife, cutting right through the skin. Place the pork belly in a roasting pan, skin side up, and set aside.

2 In a bowl, place all the marinade ingredients and mix together well. Pour the marinade over the pork belly, ensuring that it is completely covered in the marinade. Cover with plastic wrap and refrigerate for 2 hours (or overnight).

3 Remove the pork belly from the refrigerator to bring it up to room temperature 1 hour before cooking. When you are ready to cook, preheat the oven to 450°F.

4 Roast the pork in the oven for 20 minutes, then reduce the temperature to 400°F. Continue to cook for another 40 minutes, or until the skin crackles and crisps (cover with aluminum foil if it is getting too dark).

5 While the pork belly is cooking, make the red cabbage and apple slaw: In a large bowl, place all the ingredients and season with salt and black pepper. Mix very well, cover with plastic wrap, and let marinate in the refrigerator for 1 hour.

6 Once the pork belly is cooked, slice it into four pieces and place on four warm plates. Transfer the red cabbage and apple slaw to a serving bowl and place in the center of the table.

Serves 4

2¼ pounds free-range pork belly

For the marinade
3-inch piece fresh ginger, peeled and grated
2 tablespoons dark soy sauce
2 tablespoons golden Irish honey
2 red chile peppers, sliced
2 garlic cloves, peeled and sliced
1 lemongrass stalk, sliced

For the red cabbage and apple slaw
¼ red cabbage, peeled and cut into strips
1 celery stalk, thinly sliced
4 red apples, cored and cut into strips
1 carrot, peeled, halved, and cut into tstrips
⅓ cup plus 1 tablespoon mayonnaise
2 teaspoons finely chopped flat-leaf parsley
¼ cup grated fresh horseradish
sea salt and freshly ground black pepper

Free-range Pork with Apple, Cherry, and Sage Stuffing *and Apple Crisps*

Sundays were made for this… Slow-roasted juicy pork filled with apple, cherries, and sage that collect the fabulous flavors of the meat while roasting. You could substitute dates for the cherries if you wish, or use fresh flat-leaf parsley instead of the fresh sage for a more peppery flavor. Make sure to take the pork out of the refrigerator 1 hour before you intend roasting it to allow the meat to come to room temperature, which will make it more tender when cooked. The apple crisps are so simple to make and add a lovely texture to this dish.

1 Preheat the oven to 475°F. Weigh the pork before starting and make a note of its weight.

2 Start by making the stuffing: In a large bowl, place the apple, dried cherries, red onion, sage, panko bread crumbs, and melted butter. Season with salt and black pepper and mix well.

3 Butterfly the pork loin roast: Make a slit down its length, cutting just deep enough so that the loin opens up to lie flat like a book. Do not cut all the way through. Spoon the stuffing mixture onto the meat and spread evenly. Close up the loin and, using pieces of butcher's twine, tie at even intervals so that it assumes its original shape. Push in any stuffing that escapes from the ends.

4 Rub the joint all over with salt and black pepper and place in a roasting pan. Roast for 25 minutes, then reduce the heat to 350°F and cook for another 20 minutes per pound.

5 Make the apple crisps: Core the apples and slice very thinly through the middle of the apple—aim for slices that are $1/16$th inch thick. Dust with the cinnamon and lay flat on a baking sheet lined with parchment paper.

Serves 6

1 free-range boneless pork loin
    roast (about 3¼ pounds)
sea salt and freshly ground
    black pepper

For the stuffing
7 ounces baking apple, peeled,
    cored, and diced
½ cup dried cherries, coarsely
    chopped
1 red onion, peeled and finely diced
4 sage leaves, finely chopped
½ cup panko (Japanese) bread
    crumbs
3½ tablespoons butter, melted

For the apple crisps
2 baking apples
¾ tablespoon ground cinnamon

continued overleaf

Free-range Pork with Apple, Cherry, and Sage Stuffing *and Apple Crisps* continued

6 Cook in a preheated oven at 350°F for 45 minutes to 1 hour, so if you are cooking the pork at the same time, add the apple slices to the oven soon after reducing the temperature. Turn the slices halfway through and remove any crisps that have turned brown. Continue cooking until the apples have dried out and are light golden.

7 Make the apple jus: In a saucepan, combine the apples, sugar, and butter, cover, and cook gently, stirring from time to time, until the apples start to disintegrate, 15 to 20 minutes. Once the pork is cooked, pour about ½ cup of the pork cooking juices into the apples and stir.

8 Slice the roast pork and place on warmed plates. Scatter a few apple crisps over the top, and finish with a drizzle of the hot apple jus. Garnish with sage leaves and serve.

For the apple jus
2¼ pounds baking apples, peeled, cored, and coarsely chopped
2 tablespoons sugar
3½ tablespoons butter

Honey-roasted Bacon with Creamy Leeks and Cabbage

Ooh, bacon and cabbage! The culinary equivalent to a pint of Guinness in Ireland. It has got a bad rap in recent years because of the boiled bacon and over-cooked mushy cabbage that a lot of us were made to eat growing up. But cooked well, it is the most heart-warming of all dishes. The sweet glaze coating the bacon trickles through the meat as it roasts. Served up with creamed leeks and cabbage, it is pure soul food… If you prefer to just serve the honeyed bacon with plain cabbage, then cook the cabbage in the water that you boiled the bacon in—this will add lots of flavor to the cabbage.

1 Preheat the oven to 350°F.

2 Place the loin of bacon in a large saucepan and cover with cold water. Bring to a boil and let cook for 1 hour.

3 Drain off the water and transfer the bacon to a roasting pan. Using a sharp knife, remove the rind and cut crisscross lines into the fat to form a diamond pattern. Stud the fat with the cloves.

4 In a small bowl, mix together the honey and brown sugar, until you get a smooth paste. Spread this evenly over the scored fat. Roast the bacon in the oven for 30 minutes, basting every 10 minutes.

5 Remove the bacon from the oven, cover loosely with aluminum foil, and let rest for 15 minutes.

6 Carve slices of the bacon onto a warm servng plate and spoon the juices from the roasting pan over the meat. Serve with the Creamy Leeks and Cabbage.

Serves 6

4½-pound loin of bacon (cured boneless pork loin roast)
12 whole cloves
¹/₃ cup plus 1 tablespoon golden honey
1 cup light brown sugar

To serve
Creamy Leeks and Cabbage (page 187)

Butterflied Rosemary and Garlic Roast Lamb

Boned and butterflied is the fastest and easiest way to roast lamb leg. If you are not a great carver of meat roasts, you will really love this roast, as it requires slicing rather than carving. I will admit I do a lamb roast with rosemary, garlic, and red wine vinegar at least once a month at home. It's my go-to roast, tastes really good, and never fails me. Served with my Mint and Red Currant Jelly— it's so delicious. If you don't have the time to make the jelly, make a simple mint sauce (see below).

1 Preheat the oven to 425°F.

2 Make the marinade: In a bowl, place the oil, vinegar, garlic, and rosemary, season with salt and black pepper, and mix well.

3 Place the lamb, skin-side up, in a roasting pan and pour the marinade over the top. Using clean hands, rub the marinade into the lamb and let it sit for 30 minutes. This lets the flavors be absorbed into the meat and also gives the lamb time to come to room temperature before going in the oven.

4 Place the marinated lamb in the oven and roast for 40 minutes.

5 Remove the lamb from the oven, place a piece of aluminum foil loosely on top of it, and let rest for 15 minutes before you slice. Serve with Mint and Red Currant Jelly.

Serves 8

1 whole lamb leg (3¼ pounds), boned and butterflied

For the marinade
3 tablespoons olive oil
2 tablespoons red wine vinegar
3 garlic cloves, finely sliced
2 tablespoons finely chopped rosemary
sea salt and freshly ground black pepper

To serve
Mint and Red Currant Jelly (page 223)

To make a simple mint sauce, mix together ⅔ cup chopped mint, 1 teaspoon sugar, 1 tablespoon hot water, and 2 tablespoons white wine vinegar. Let stand for 20 minutes before serving to let the flavors infuse.

Slow-roasted Lamb Shanks *with* *Creamy Ginger Potatoes*

Lamb shanks, when cooked slowly on low heat, become so tender and juicy. You do need to prop them with lots of flavorsome ingredients, and I love these sweet and spicy cinnamon, chile, honey, and Marsala flavors with mine. The ginger creamy potatoes add both soft texture and a subtle zing.

1 Preheat the oven to 300°F.

2 Place a casserole dish over medium heat and pour in the olive oil. Stir in the onion, sweet potatoes, cinnamon, red pepper flakes, ground ginger, and garlic, cover the pan, and simmer for 5 minutes. Remove the ingredients from the pan and set aside.

3 Add the lamb shanks to the casserole dish and brown them on each side. Season with salt and black pepper. Return the onion, sweet potatoes, and spices to the casserole, followed by 2 cups water, the honey, and Marsala. Stir, cover the pan, and bring to a boil.

4 Transfer the casserole dish to the oven and cook for 2 hours.

5 While the lamb is cooking, make the creamy ginger potatoes: Place the potatoes, whole and unpeeled, in a large saucepan with the largest potatoes at the bottom. Fill the pan halfway with water, cover, and place over high heat. When the water starts to boil, drain off half, leaving just enough for the potatoes to steam.

6 When the potatoes are cooked, about 30 to 40 minutes depending on their size, drain and peel (hold them in a kitchen towel if they are too hot to handle), then place in a warm bowl.

7 In a saucepan, combine the milk, butter, and fresh ginger. Heat over low heat, stirring, until the milk has warmed through and the butter melted.

8 Pour the warm ginger milk into the warm potatoes, season with salt and black pepper, and mash well.

9 Spoon the creamy ginger potatoes onto two warm plates and place the lamb shanks with the sauce on top.

Serves 2

2 tablespoons olive oil
1 onion, peeled and finely chopped
2 medium sweet potatoes, peeled and diced
1 teaspoon ground cinnamon
1 teaspoon dried red pepper flakes
2 teaspoons ground ginger
2 garlic cloves, peeled and crushed
4 medium-size lamb shanks
sea salt and freshly ground black pepper
2 tablespoons golden honey
3 tablespoons Marsala wine

For the potatoes
1 pound Yukon Gold potatoes
¼ cup plus 2 tablespoons milk
2 tablespoons butter
1 teaspoon grated fresh ginger
sea salt and freshly ground black pepper

Celery Root and Potato *Gratin*

I have a great love affair with celery root–there is so much you can do with it and it has a wonderful nutty flavor. Peel and slice it into thin strips, mix it with coarse-grain mustard and mayonnaise, and you have celery root rémoulade, which is delicious served with cold meats or roast beef. This gratin could be served on its own, perhaps with the addition of spicy sausage or diced bacon, but I love to serve it alongside any roast of meat. You could add a sprinkle of mature Cheddar, Gouda or Parmesan to the cream mixture.

1 Preheat the oven to 350°F.

2 Grease a 1-quart baking dish with butter and sprinkle the crushed garlic over the bottom of the dish.

3 Bring a large saucepan of water to a boil. Drop the sliced potatoes and celery root into the boiling water and cook for 5 minutes, then drain and arrange in layers in the dish, overlapping the slices slightly and seasoning each layer with salt and black pepper

4 In a small bowl, beat together the milk and half and half and pour over the vegetables. Use your hand to push down the potatoes and celery root until they are completely immersed in the milk and cream mixture. Sprinkle the nutmeg over the top and cover with parchment paper.

5 Roast in the oven for 30 minutes, then remove the parchment paper, increase the heat to 400°F, and bake for another 20 minutes, or until the top is golden.

Serves 4–6

6 tablespoons butter, softened, plus
  extra for greasing
2 garlic cloves, peeled and crushed
2 pounds potatoes, peeled and
  thinly sliced
18 ounces celery root (celeriac),
  peeled, quartered, and
  thinly sliced
sea salt and freshly ground
  black pepper
1 cup milk
1 cup half and half
½ teaspoon freshly grated nutmeg

Cauliflower Cheese *with Hazelnut Topping*

This is delicious served with any roast, as the creaminess is perfect with meats, and it acts as a sauce as well as a vegetable. Try to use a mature Cheddar as it will add a richer flavor to the dish. The hazelnut topping adds a crunchy texture and tastes great. You could use half cauliflower and half broccoli in this recipe for variety.

1 Preheat the oven to 325°F. Lightly grease a gratin dish.

2 Remove the outer leaves from the cauliflower and coarsely chop. Then place the cauliflower and leaves in a saucepan with about a 1-inch depth of water. Cook on medium heat for 10 minutes (you want the cauliflower slightly undercooked, as it will be cooked in the oven also).

3 Meanwhile, in a separate saucepan, melt the butter and beat in the flour. Cook for 2 to 3 minutes, stirring continuously. Then add the milk, beating continuously to ensure that no lumps form, and cook for a few minutes, until thickened. Stir in the shredded cheese and the freshly grated nutmeg.

4 Drain the cauliflower, place in the greased dish, and pour over the cheese sauce.

5 Next, make the hazelnut topping: Place the hazelnuts on a baking tray and roast them in the oven for 10 minutes. Once roasted, remove from the oven (leave it on) and place the hazelnuts in a food processor. Blend for 30 seconds (you don't want them too fine), then mix them together with the Parmesan cheese and bread crumbs and season. Sprinkle the hazelnut topping over the cauliflower cheese.

6 Bake in the preheated oven for 20 minutes, until bubbling, then serve immediately.

Serves 4 as a side dish

1 small cauliflower
5½ tablespoons butter, plus more
  for greasing
²/₃ cup all-purpose flour
1²/₃ cups milk
1 cup shredded sharp Irish
  Cheddar cheese
1 teaspoon freshly grated nutmeg

For the topping
¹/₃ cup hazelnuts
¹/₃ cup Parmesan cheese
1½ cups bread crumbs
sea salt and freshly ground
  black pepper

Slow-cooked Red Cabbage with Apples and Golden Raisins

Red cabbage is so good for you, and it's absolutely delicious when you slow cook it with apples and golden raisins. I place the apples on the top because, as the dish cooks, the apples break down and the juices run through the red cabbage. This recipe looks stunning and is so good served with beef, pork, or turkey, as it brings moisture and a sweet flavor. You can make it a couple of days in advance, and if you don't eat it all in one sitting, it's great cold in sandwiches with grilled chicken or turkey.

1 Preheat the oven to 300°F.

2 Arrange a layer of the shredded cabbage in the base of a casserole dish and season lightly with sea salt and black pepper. Add a layer of chopped apples with a sprinkling of nutmeg, sugar, sliced shallots, and golden raisins. Continue layering up the red cabbage and apple in this way until everything is used up. Pour in the vinegar and dot with butter on top.

3 Cover the casserole dish with a tight-fitting lid and let cook very slowly in the oven for 2 to 2¼ hours, stirring once or twice during cooking.

Serves 10

2 pounds red cabbage, shredded (discard the tough outer leaves)
sea salt and freshly ground black pepper
1 pound baking apples, peeled, cored, and finely chopped
¼ whole nutmeg, freshly grated
3 tablespoons dark brown sugar
2 shallots, peeled and finely sliced
⅔ cup golden raisins
3 tablespoons sherry wine vinegar
2 heaping tablespoons butter

Beet and Horseradish Cream

I love to serve this with my Cork Spiced Beef (page 164).

1 In a bowl, mix together all of the ingredients and season to taste with sea salt and black pepper.

Serves 10

1 beet, boiled, peeled, and grated
2-inch piece fresh horseradish, grated
5 tablespoons crème fraîche
juice of 1 lemon
sea salt and freshly ground black pepper

Perfect Roast Potatoes

I have tried many ingredients and methods to perfect the roast potato and I have found no better result than using goose fat. Goose fat has become one of those essential Christmas or Sunday roast ingredients. It does have a wonderful silky, buttery texture, and adds real depth and flavor to potatoes, as well as creating that delicious crispy potato skin that we all love. You can substitute rosemary for the thyme, if you prefer.

1 Preheat the oven to 400°F.

2 Cut the potatoes in half, or into quarters if they are very big—they should all be similar in size. Put them in a saucepan of cold salted water, bring to a boil, and cook for 8 minutes. Drain.

3 Place the goose fat in a roasting pan over a hot stove. When the goose fat is hot, stir in the thyme leaves and whole cloves of garlic, which add a subtle flavor. Add the potatoes and season with salt and black pepper. Toss the potatoes in the fat and then place in the oven for 30 minutes. As the potatoes roast, baste in the goose fat every 10 minutes.

Serves 6

4 pounds potatoes (Yukon Gold or russet), peeled
3 tablespoons goose fat
3 tablespoons chopped thyme leaves
2 garlic cloves, peeled and left whole
sea salt and freshly ground black pepper

Creamed Potatoes 5 Ways

Mash, pandy (as my dad would call it), puréed... We have so many names for creamed potatoes in Ireland because we love them, and we all have our own great way of making them. Have fun trying all the different ways to serve creamed, mashed, pandy, and puréed potatoes!

1 Place the potatoes, whole and unpeeled, in a saucepan with the largest ones at the bottom, and fill the pan halfway with water. Cover the pan and place over high heat. When the water begins to boil, drain off about half of it, leaving just enough for the potatoes to steam.

2 When the potatoes are cooked, about 30 to 40 minutes depending on their size, drain and peel (hold them in a kitchen towel if they are too hot to handle), then place in a warm bowl.

3 Mash the potatoes, gradually adding the warm milk. Then add the nutmeg, and butter, and season to taste with salt and black pepper.

Serves 4

2¼ pounds Yukon Gold potatoes
⅓ cup warm milk
¼ teaspoon freshly grated nutmeg
3½ tablespoons butter
sea salt and freshly ground
    black pepper

Variations

Mustard Creamed Potatoes
Fold in 1 tablespoon dry mustard and 1 tablespoon yellow mustard seeds.

Colcannon
Add 2 chopped scallions or 1 finely chopped leek to the cold milk in a saucepan and slowly warm the milk while cooking the scallions or leeks.

Sweet Onion Creamed Potatoes
Stir in 6 tablespoons caramelized onions.

Cheddar Cheese Creamed Potatoes
Stir in 6 tablespoons shredded sharp Cheddar.

St. Patrick's Creamed Potatoes
And for all you fun-loving St. Patrick's Day followers, add in 4 tablespoons finely chopped flat-leaf parsley for the green effect!

When choosing potatoes, the more floury types work best, because they cream more easily. Cooking the potatoes in their skins keeps in all the delicious flavors and nutrients. It also allows the butter and milk to be easily absorbed once you do peel them, ensuring a wonderful, smooth mash.

Garden Herbed Hasselback Potatoes

Cutting slits in the potatoes is not just to make the potato look better, I do it so that the aromatic flavors of the fresh herbs and garlic seep right into the potato. I love this way of roasting potatoes—they look lovely, the texture is great and the flavor is superb. You could use hot goose fat instead of butter for extra flavor. Below are my favorite herbs to use for this recipe, but if you grow herbs at home, just use whatever you have that is fresh. Pictured on page 154.

1 Preheat the oven to 400°F.

2 Cut into each potato at about 1/8-inch intervals, without cutting all the way through, so that they resemble mini toast racks. Then drop them into a saucepan of boiling water over medium heat and simmer for about 5 minutes.

3 While the potatoes are simmering, in a bowl, combine the finely chopped herbs, sea salt, and crushed garlic.

4 Place a medium-size saucepan over low heat. Add the butter and stir until melted. Add the olive oil and herb mix and stir well until combined.

5 Drain the potatoes and toss them in the herb and butter mixture, making sure they are well coated.

6 Place a roasting pan over medium heat and transfer the herbed potatoes, along with any juices, to the pan. Turn the potatoes in the herbed butter, cut side down first, then turn them so that they are cut side up. Spoon the juices over them.

7 Place in the oven and roast for 15 to 20 minutes, until tender and browned.

Serves 6

24 new potatoes
7 tablespoons butter
2 tablespoons olive oil

For the garden herb mixture
2 teaspoons finely chopped
   fresh thyme
1 teaspoon finely chopped
   fresh rosemary
1 teaspoon finely chopped
   fresh marjoram
1 teaspoon finely chopped
   fresh flat-leaf parsley
1/3 cup sea salt
2 garlic cloves, crushed

Smoked Bacon *Stuffins*

I came up with this recipe a few years ago, as sometimes stuffing can look very messy on a plate, but these stuffins are gorgeous and taste as good as they look. They look like muffins made of stuffing, hence why I came up with the name "stuffin." You can prepare these the day before and they also freeze very well. If you are throwing a party, you can make mini versions—they make great hot canapés.

1 Preheat the oven to 350°F. Lightly grease an 8-cup mini muffin pan.

2 In a bowl, place the bread crumbs, shallots, garlic, pine nuts, parsley, sage, lemon zest, and softened butter. Season with sea salt and black pepper and mix well to combine.

3 Prepare the bacon slices: Stretch each one out out using the back of a knife so that it gets longer and thinner. Then line each cup of the muffin pan with two bacon slices.

4 Fill each one with the bread crumb mixture. Press the filling in firmly with the back of a spoon so that it does not crumble when it comes out of the oven.

5 Bake in the oven for 10 minutes, or until the bacon is crispy and the stuffing is cooked through.

Makes 8

3$\frac{1}{4}$ cups fresh bread crumbs
2 shallots, peeled and finely diced
1 garlic clove, peeled and crushed
$\frac{1}{3}$ cup pine nuts, toasted and chopped
1 tablespoon finely chopped flat-leaf parsley
1 tablespoon finely chopped sage
2 teaspoons finely grated lemon zest
7 tablespoons butter, softened, plus extra for greasing
sea salt and freshly ground black pepper
16 smoked bacon slices

Honey-glazed *Vegetables*

Honey mixed with melted butter, mustard, and brown sugar creates the perfect glaze for root vegetables. You could substitute the honey and brown sugar with maple syrup if you wish. I also sometimes add a sprinkle of sesame seeds over the vegetables before I put them in the oven for a crunchy texture. You could use butternut squash, turnip, or celery root in this dish too.

1 Preheat the oven to 325°F. Place the carrots and parsnips in a roasting pan or ovenproof dish along with the whole scallions.

2 In a small saucepan, melt the butter over low heat and stir in the honey, Dijon mustard, and brown sugar.

3 Drizzle the warmed honey and butter mixture over the vegetables and toss to make sure they are well coated. Season with sea salt and black pepper.

4 Roast in the oven for 40 minutes, stirring occasionally to coat the vegetables evenly with the glaze. Serve hot.

Serves 4

2 carrots, peeled and chopped into wedges
2 parsnips, peeled and chopped into wedges
4 scallions, left whole
3½ tablespoons butter
1 tablespoon golden honey
1 teaspoon Dijon mustard
1 tablespoon light brown sugar
sea salt and freshly ground black pepper

Even though, to my mind,
we still grow the best potatoes
in the world, we are no longer
just a nation of potato growers.
You'll find farmers' markets
and vegetable stores in Ireland
packed with seasonal varieties
from squashes to kales,
heirloom tomatoes, celery root
and more.

Creamy Leeks and Cabbage

I love to serve this with my Honey-roasted Bacon on page 170.

1 In a saucepan over medium heat, heat the butter. Once it has melted, stir in the garlic, leeks and cabbage and season with salt and black pepper. Cover and cook for 5 minutes.

2 Remove the lid and cook, uncovered and stirring, until softened, another 2 minutes. Stir in the half and half and nutmeg and season again. Cook for 5 minutes more, stirring every minute, then serve.

Serves 4

3½ tablespoons butter
2 garlic cloves, crushed
2 leeks, thinly sliced
1 head savoy cabbage, shredded
sea salt and freshly ground
    black pepper
¾ cup plus 1 tablespoon half
    and half
¼ teaspoon freshly grated nutmeg

Celery Root and Hazelnut *Purée*

Creamed celery root is one of my favorite things to eat, and the addition of hazelnuts makes it even better. If you have time, pop the hazelnuts in a hot oven for 10 minutes to roast–this will strenghten the flavor. This purée is perfect to serve with any roast, but you could also serve it with beef tenderloin, wild game, meaty fish, or a grilled breast of chicken.

1 In a large saucepan, place the celery root and cover with cold water. Place over high heat and bring to a boil. Once the water has started boiling, reduce the heat to a simmer and cook for 15 minutes, or until the celery root is tender.

2 Meanwhile, in a food processor, finely grind the hazelnuts.

3 In a saucepan, combine the butter and half and half and gently warm over low heat, until the butter has melted into the cream. Pour over the cooked celery root and season with salt and black pepper. Mash or beat together well, then fold the ground hazelnuts through the puréed celery root.

Serves 4

1½ pounds celery root (celeriac),
    peeled and cut into chunks
¾ cup whole skinned hazelnuts
3½ tablespoons butter
½ cup half and half
sea salt and freshly ground
    black pepper

THE *Sweetest* THING

Irish Honey, Orange, and Pistachio *Florentines*

These are sweet and crunchy, and delicious served after dinner with coffee. You could also make a dessert out of them by sticking them on top of a scoop of my Baileys Soda Bread Ice Cream (page 211), like butterfly wings. You could substitute hazelnuts or pecans for the pistachios. They also make great edible gifts; stack them in a cellophane bag, tied with a ribbon.

1 Preheat the oven to 350°F and line 2 baking sheets with parchment paper.

2 In a large mixing bowl, place the chopped pistachios, flour, and orange zest and stir together.

3 In a small saucepan, place the sugar, butter, honey, and cream, stir together, and bring to a boil over medium heat, until all the ingredients are melted and well combined.

4 Next, stir the hot butter mixture into the pistachio mixture. Mix well to combine.

5 Using a spoon, drop a heaping teaspoonful of the batter onto one of the prepared baking sheets, and use the back of the spoon to flatten it out into a disk. Repeat with the remaining batter over both baking sheets. Leave space in between each Florentine, as the batter will spread.

6 Bake in the oven for 8 minutes.

7 Once they are baked, let the cookies cool before removing them from the baking sheets.

These will keep for up to 5 days in an airtight container.

Makes 24

1 cup finely chopped pistachios
$^1/_3$ cup all-purpose flour
zest of 2 oranges
$^1/_4$ cup sugar
3$^1/_2$ tablespoons butter
$^1/_4$ cup golden honey
1 tablespoon half and half

Marmalade and Cardamom *Pudding*

Marmalade pudding was a favorite in Irish households for generations, but in recent years it has been forgotten. I am not sure why, but I am hoping that it will have a revival. The flavors of cardamom and orange are so good together–if you haven't used cardamom seeds before, now is the time to try them. The seeds are contained in small green pods and they have a wonderful aroma and an enticing warm, spicy–sweet flavor. You only use the seeds in this recipe, and you will need about five pods to get one teaspoon of seeds. Don't discard the shells after you take out the seeds–instead, add them to a jar of superfine sugar, give a good shake, and you'll have a wonderful cardamom-infused sugar, beautiful for baking or making a syrup.

1 Lightly grease a 1-quart steam bowl.

2 In a large mixing bowl, cream the butter and sugar until light and fluffy, then beat in the eggs, followed by the marmalade and ground cardamom seeds.

3 Sift the flour and baking powder into the bowl and mix together with a wooden spoon. Stir in the milk to loosen the batter.

4 In a small bowl, mix together the syrup and orange zest.

5 Using a pastry brush, glaze the inside of the greased bowl with the syrup and orange zest mixture. Pour the batter into the bowl, tightly cover with a circle of wax paper, and secure around the rim of the bowl with kitchen string. Place the pudding basin in the center of a large saucepan and fill the saucepan with hot water to about three-quarters up the side of the bowl. Cover the pan with the lid, place over medium heat, and steam the pudding until a skewer inserted in the center comes out clean, about 1½ hours, topping up the water if necessary.

6 Remove the paper cover and invert the pudding onto a serving plate. Serve with cream or my Homemade Custard (page 201).

Serves 6

7 tablespoons butter, plus more for greasing
½ cup plus 1 tablespoon superfine sugar
2 large free-range eggs
3 tablespoons marmalade
1 teaspoon cardamom seeds, ground
¾ cup plus 2 tablespoons all-purpose flour
1 teaspoon baking powder
1 tablespoon milk
⅓ cup plus 1 tablespoon golden syrup or dark corn syrup
zest of 1 orange

Rhubarb and Ginger *Cheesecake*

Layers of aromatic crunchy ginger cookies, tangy rhubarb, and a soft, silky cream cheese topping make this my favorite cheesecake. You could replace the rhubarb with strawberries, nectarines, plums, or raspberries—if you are doing so, change the cookies to suit the fruit. You could also mix hazelnuts or almonds with graham crackers for the base. You can make this cheesecake a day in advance, but take it out of the refrigerator an hour before serving to take the chill out of it.

1 Start by making the roasted rhubarb. Preheat the oven to 350°F.

2 Arrange the rhubarb pieces in a roasting pan in a single layer. Sprinkle the sugar on top and drizzle over 1/3 cup water.

3 Roast for 10 minutes, then remove from the oven and let cool.

4 Next, make the cookie crumb crust. Lightly grease an 8-inch springform or tart pan. In a small saucepan, melt the butter over medium heat. In a food processor, blitz the cookies until finely crushed and transfer to a bowl. Pour the melted butter over the crumbs and mix well. Press the crumb mixture into the prepared pan. Refrigerate for 30 minutes, or until firm and cold.

5 In a large bowl, beat together the cream cheese and superfine sugar, until the sugar has dissolved and the mixture is smooth.

6 In a separate bowl, whip the cream until stiff peaks form and then fold it into the cream cheese mixture.

7 Arrange the roasted rhubarb pieces in a single layer on the chilled cookie crumb crust, reserving the syrup for serving.

8 Spread the cream cheese mixture on top and let set in the fridge overnight, or for at least 3 hours, before serving.

9 Drizzle with the reserved rhubarb syrup for serving.

Serves 8

7 tablespoons butter, plus extra for greasing
5 ounces gingersnaps
1½ cups cream cheese
¾ cup superfine sugar
1¼ cups heavy cream

For the roasted rhubarb
1¼ pounds rhubarb, chopped into 4-inch pieces
½ cup sugar

Salted Caramel Whisky Bread and Butter Pudding
with Golden Raisins

You could say that I grew up on bread and butter pudding. My mum or dad would prepare it at least once every two weeks. It is so simple to make and great for using up stale bread. I believe that it can also be a very elegant dish —in fact, I served this very recipe at my pop-up restaurant in NYC a few years back, and it was the most requested dessert on the menu. I wasn't surprised! The salted caramel whiskey sauce is addictive and could also be poured over ice cream to make an Irish sundae. This pudding can be made up to a day in advance and warmed through in the oven before serving.

1 Preheat the oven to 400°F and grease an 8½-inch square nonreactive baking dish.

2 In a medium-size mixing bowl, combine the golden raisins and whiskey and let soak for 1 hour.

3 In a large bowl, beat together the eggs, cream, sugar, spices, and vanilla to make a custard. Spread one side of each slice of bread with the butter. Cut the slices in half diagonally and arrange half of the bread in the bottom of the baking dish, overlapping the slices. Drain the raisins and sprinkle half over the bread. Repeat with the remaining bread and raisins. Pour the custard over the bread and let soak for 30 minutes.

4 Place the baking dish in a large baking pan. Add enough hot water to come halfway up the sides of the dish. Bake in the oven for 50 to 60 minutes, or until the pudding is set and the top is golden. Remove the baking dish from the water bath and let cool slightly on a wire rack.

5 Make the salted caramel whiskey sauce: In a small saucepan, melt the butter over medium heat. Beat in the sugar, sea salt, cream, and whiskey. Reduce the heat to low and simmer until the sauce thickens, about 10 minutes. Serve the pudding warm with the salted caramel whiskey sauce spooned over each serving.

Serves 6

²/₃ cup golden raisins
½ cup Irish whiskey
5 extra-large eggs
2 cups heavy cream
1 cup plus 2 tablespoons sugar
½ teaspoon ground cinnamon
¼ teaspoon ground nutmeg
1 teaspoon vanilla extract
8 to 9 slices firm white bread, crusts left on
3½ sticks unsalted butter, at room temperature, plus more for greasing

For the salted caramel whiskey sauce
1 stick unsalted butter, cut into pieces
1 cup plus 2 tablespoons sugar
2 teaspoons sea salt
2½ cups heavy cream
¼ cup Irish whiskey

Apple and Lavender *Topless Tart*

This tart looks so pretty with the caramelized apples glimmering up at you. The lavender creates a deep, aromatic flavor, that is so good with the sweet apples.

1 Make the pie crust: In a food processor, place the flour, sugar, and salt and process for a few seconds to combine. Add the chilled butter and pulse until the mixture resembles bread crumbs–this should take about 10 seconds. With the food processor still running, add the ice water in a slow, steady stream through the feed tube, until the dough just holds together.

2 Turn the dough out onto a lightly floured work surface. Divide in two, place each half on a sheet of plastic wrap, and cover with another sheet of plastic wrap. Flatten using a rolling pin and form two disks. Wrap and refrigerate for at least 1 hour before using.

3 Preheat the oven to 400°F. Mix the sugar with the lavender flowers and let infuse while you prepare the apples.

4 Peel, halve, and core the apples. Reserve one of the apple halves, and halve all the others again into quarters. Place all the apples in a bowl and squeeze over the lemon juice. Toss gently.

5 Place an 8-inch heavy-bottomed ovenproof skillet over high heat. Add the lavender-infused sugar along with 3 tablespoons water. Bring to a boil, then reduce the heat to medium. Continue to cook until thickened and syrupy. Remove from the heat and stir in the butter.

6 Place the reserved apple half in the center of the skillet and arrange the apple quarters around it, cut side up. Place the skillet back over medium heat for about 5 minutes

7 Remove the chilled dough from the refrigerator and roll out to a circle slightly larger all around than your skillet. Place the dough over the apples and syrup and tuck in the edges. Pop the tart into the oven for 30 to 35 minutes, until the crust is golden brown.

8 Remove from the oven and let cool for 5 minutes, then place a plate, slightly larger than the pan, on top. Invert the tart onto the plate. Serve warm with softly whipped cream.

Serves 6

For the pie crust
2²/₃ cups all-purpose flour,
    plus more for flouring
1 teaspoon sugar
1 teaspoon salt
2 sticks unsalted butter, chilled and
    cubed
¹/₃ cup plus 1 tablespoon ice water

For the topping
1 cup sugar
2 teaspoons dried lavender flowers
8 medium apples
juice of 1 lemon
3½ tablespoons butter

There is no better way to welcome someone into your home than with a slice of home baked apple tart and a freshly brewed cup of tea

Irish Apple Tart

Thin, buttery pie crust, soft, sugary apples, and softly whipped cream… Even the mention of apple tart gives me comfort. Everyone in Ireland has their favorite recipe and enough anecdotes to go with it to fill numerous books! My mom makes the best apple tart. When I was growing up, she would always make it on Sundays after mass. I would sit at the kitchen table as a child and peel the apples while watching her make the pie crust, crumbling the butter and flour between her fingers and humming along to RTÉ radio in the background. I love this memory as much as I love the apple tart itself.

1 First, make the pie crust: Using a stand mixer, cream together the butter and sugar. Add the eggs and beat for several minutes. Reduce the speed to low and mix in the flour. Turn out onto a floured board and shape into a ball. Wrap in plastic wrap and chill in the refrigerator. This dough needs to be chilled for at least 1 hour, otherwise it is difficult to handle.

2 Preheat the oven to 350°F. Lightly grease a 9-inch pan.

3 Make the tart: Roll out the dough on a lightly floured work surface to a thickness of approximately 1/8 inch. Use about two-thirds of the dough to line the prepared pan.

4 Place the diced apples in the pastry shell and sprinkle with the sugar and cinnamon. Cover with the remaining dough to form a lid. Press down the edges to seal and, using a small knife, make little slits in the top.

5 Mix the beaten egg with the milk to make an egg wash. Brush the top of the pie with the egg wash and then bake in the preheated oven for 45 minutes to 1 hour, until the apples are tender.

6 Once cooked, remove from the oven and sprinkle with superfine sugar while it's still hot. Let cool on a wire rack. Serve warm with softly whipped cream or vanilla ice cream.

Serves 8

For the pie crust
2 sticks butter, softened, plus more for greasing
1/4 cup superfine sugar
2 large free-range eggs
2¾ cups all-purpose flour, plus more for flouring

For the filling
1½ pounds baking apples, peeled, cored, and diced
scant ¾ cup granulated sugar
1 teaspoon ground cinnamon
1 large egg, beaten
splash of milk
superfine sugar, for sprinkling

Ginger and Date Treacle Pudding

This is one of my favorite desserts to make when I need a little comfort or sweetening. The rich dates and golden syrup make this pudding decadent, and the ginger brings it to life. You could make these in individual pudding bowls if you wish. I like to serve this pudding with softly whipped heavy cream or vanilla ice cream, or my Salted Caramel Whiskey Sauce.

Serves 6

2 ounces Medjool dates, pitted and coarsely chopped

2 teaspoons ground ginger

1 stick butter, plus more for greasing

¼ cup packed dark brown sugar

5 tablespoons superfine sugar

2 large free-range eggs

4 tablespoons golden syrup or dark corn syrup, plus (optional) more to serve

2 tablespoons molasses

2½ cups all-purpose flour

2 teaspoons baking powder

2 tablespoons milk

1 Lightly grease a 1-quart steam bowl.

2 In a food processor, blitz the dates with the ground ginger for 1 minute, then set aside.

3 In a large bowl, cream together the butter and brown and white sugars until light and fluffy. Beat in the eggs, followed by the date and ground ginger mixture, the syrup, and the molasses.

4 Next, sift the flour and baking powder into the bowl and stir in with a wooden spoon. Stir in the milk to loosen the batter.

5 Pour the batter into the greased bowl, tightly cover with a circle of wax paper, and secure around the rim of the bowl with kitchen string. Place the bowl in the center of a large saucepan and fill the saucepan with hot water to about three-quarters up the side of the bowl. Cover the pan with the lid, place over medium heat, and steam the pudding for 2 hours, topping up the water if necessary.

6 Remove the paper cover and invert the pudding onto a serving plate. Serve with cream and extra syrup poured over the pudding, or my Salted Caramel Whiskey Sauce (page 194).

Spiced Baked Apples *with Homemade Custard*

These were my dad's speciality—nobody could ever make them like he could and he loved that fact! But I watched how he made them and I am carrying on his wonderful recipe. I love to make these on Sundays after a roast or as a mid-week treat. They look so fabulous, and the flavors of honey, cinnamon, and cloves infuse the whole apple. If you don't have time to make the custard, serve with softly whipped cream or ice cream.

1 Preheat the oven to 350°F.

2 Remove the cores of the apples with an apple corer. Using a spoon, enlarge the size of the cavity so that it is doubled in size. Arrange the apples in a baking dish.

3 In a small bowl, place the brown sugar, honey, cinnamon, and melted butter and mix together. Pour the thick liquid into the cores of each apple.

4 Pierce each apple with 4 cloves around its diameter. Bake the apples in the oven for 30 minutes.

5 While the apples are baking, make the custard: In a saucepan, place the milk over medium heat and add the vanilla bean. Let infuse over the heat until just boiling.

6 In a bowl, mix together the egg yolks, superfine sugar, and cornstarch, until a smooth paste. Pour in the vanilla-infused milk and stir well. Remove the vanilla bean, wash, and dry to reuse in another recipe. Strain the mixture back into a clean saucepan and cook gently, stirring continuously, until the custard thickens.

7 Pour the custard over the apples just before you serve.

Serves 4

4 baking apples
2/3 cup light brown sugar
3 tablespoons golden honey
4 teaspoons ground cinnamon
5½ tablespoons butter, melted
16 whole cloves

For the custard
1 2/3 cups milk
1 vanilla bean
3 large free-range egg yolks
1 tablespoon. plus ½ teaspoon
   superfine sugar
1 teaspoon cornstarch

Wild Elderflower *Gelatin Desserts*

This is such a decadent dessert. Light and subtle in flavor, it makes a great palate cleanser after fish or a rich meal. The flavor of elderflower is floral and fragrant, subtle yet full, not sweet, but heaven in a glass when infused in a light sugar syrup or set in a jelly like this one. Elderflowers grow wild in Ireland during the month of June, so when you are out walking in the country roads, keep an eye out for them as you may be walking past one of the most delightful wild ingredients that will make a delicious gelatin dessert or cordial.

1 Place the sugar and 1¾ cups water in a saucepan over medium heat and bring to a boil. Keep stirring until the sugar has dissolved, then remove from the heat.

2 Soak the gelatin sheets in a bowl of cold water until soft, about 1 minute. Drain and stir into the syrup, until dissolved.

3 Add the elderflower cordial to the sugar syrup. Stir gently to combine, then let cool.

4 Divide the cooled gelatin syrup among 4 individual 7 fl oz glasses and refrigerate until set, about 1 hour.

Serves 4

¾ cup superfine sugar
4 gelatin sheets
⅔ cups Wild Elderflower Cordial
   (see page 215)

Raspberries are also delicious added to this jelly. Simply place 1⅔ cups raspberries in the glasses (divided evenly) and pour the gelatin syrup into the glasses as above.

Rose Water-infused Carrageen Moss
with Rhubarb Compote

Carrageen moss is a red seaweed found on the West and South coasts of Ireland. The seaweed has been used in recipes for years in Ireland as a natural thickening agent. It has a very subtle sea flavor, and you can find it in health stores, where it is sold in dried form. This pudding is light and fluffy, sweetened by the delicate rose water and lifted by the tangy rhubarb compote. It's perfect to serve as a dessert after fish as it cleanses the palate. If you are unable to get your hands on rose water, you can just leave it out.

1 In a bowl, soak the moss in lukewarm water for 15 minutes. Drain and place the moss in a saucepan with the milk, rose water, vanilla bean, and 1 tablespoon of the sugar. Bring to a boil, then reduce the heat and simmer until the mixture thickens to the consistency of yogurt, about 30 minutes.

2 Pour through a strainer into a bowl, pushing the natural gelatin from the moss through the strainer.

3 Place the egg yolks in a separate bowl and beat in the remaining 3 tablespoons sugar. Beat in the strained milk mixture.

4 In another bowl, beat the egg whites until they form stiff peaks, then fold them into the mixture with a metal spoon. Use a figure-of-eight motion to get rid of any blobs of egg white.

5 Fill six small pots with the mixture, cover with plastic wrap, and refrigerate until set, about 1 hour.

6 Make the rhubarb compote: In a saucepan, heat the sugar with 1 tablespoon water and then add the rhubarb. Let simmer gently for 3 to 4 minutes.

7 Serve the rose water pots with the rhubarb compote on top.

Serves 6

1 cup dry Irish (carrageen) moss
3 cups milk
1 teaspoon rose water
1 vanilla bean
4 tablespoons sugar
2 large eggs, separated

For the rhubarb compote
1/3 cup sugar
9½ ounces rhubarb, chopped

Individual Raspberry and Baileys *Trifles*

One of my favorite desserts when I lived in Italy was a tiramisu, and in Ireland during the Christmas period we traditionally make a sherry trifle. So I have taken both desserts and made my kind of Irish trifle that I love to eat all year round–creamy layers with sweet, plump raspberries and the deep flavors of coffee and Baileys. You can make one big fabulous bowl to create oohs and aahs at the table, or more sophisticated individual portions in your best glasses.

Serves 4

3 large free-range egg yolks
5½ tablespoons superfine sugar
1⅓ cups mascarpone cheese
⅓ cup plus 1 tablespoon Baileys Irish cream liqueur
⅓ cup plus 1 tablespoon cold strong coffee or espresso
14 ladyfingers
¾ cup fresh raspberries
scant ½ cup unsweetened cocoa powder
3½ ounces white chocolate, grated

1 In a large bowl, using a handheld electric mixer, beat the egg yolks and sugar together, until pale and thick.

2 Add the mascarpone cheese and beat slowly, until the mixture is pale and smooth. Stir in the Baileys liqueur and 3 tablespoons of the coffee.

3 Dip half of the ladyfingers into the remaining coffee, then place in the bottom of four glasses or small bowls. Alternatively, put the ingredients in a single glass bowl to make one large dessert.

4 Spoon over half of the Baileys and mascarpone mixture, then half of the raspberries, followed by half of the cocoa. Repeat with another layer of ladyfingers, mascarpone, raspberries, and cocoa, then sprinkle the grated white chocolate on top.

5 Refrigerate the trifles until set, 2 hours.

Irish Coffee Chocolate Mousse

Light, airy and silky chocolate mousse infused with coffee and whiskey, and topped with softly whipped cream. This mousse is very simple and fast to prepare, and in this simplicity lies its greatness.

1 In a saucepan over low heat, combine the chocolate, coffee, and whiskey and heat, stirring continuously, until melted. Remove from the heat and let cool.

2 In a large bowl, beat the egg whites until they are stiff, then set aside. In a separate bowl, beat two of the egg yolks (use the other two in another recipe) with the sugar, then stir in the chocolate, whiskey, and coffee mixture, until smooth.

3 Gently fold in the egg whites, then pour the mixture into six small clear glasses and refrigerate until set, about 2 hours or, even better, overnight. Just before serving, spoon a layer of whipped cream on top of the chocolate mousses.

Serves 6

9 ounces semisweet chocolate, broken into pieces
$^1/_3$ cup plus 1 tablespoon strong espresso coffee
3½ tablespoons Irish whiskey
4 large free-range eggs, separated
2½ tablespoons light muscovado or Barbados sugar
½ cup half and half, whipped, to serve

How to make Irish Coffee

An Irish coffee is a classic Irish after-dinner drink, when everyone is so full they might roll over – it brings the party back to where it started!

1 Warm a wine glass by placing a spoon in the glass and filling the glass with boiling water (the spoon stops the glass from breaking). Let stand for 1 minute and then drain the water.

2 Pour the hot coffee into the wine glass to fill it just over halfway.

3 Add the brown sugar and stir until it has completely dissolved. Then stir in the Irish whiskey.

4 Slowly pour the heavy cream over the back of a teaspoon held at the surface of the coffee so that the cream floats on top of the coffee. Serve immediately.

Serves 1

$^2/_3$ cup hot freshly brewed coffee
1 teaspoon light brown sugar
2 tablespoons Irish whiskey
3½ tablespoons heavy cream

To make a Baileys Irish Coffee, add 2 tablespoons Baileys Irish cream liqueur instead of the whiskey.

Irish Affogato with Whiskey and Honey Ice Cream

An affogato is a scoop of ice cream with espresso poured over it. I loved making this when I lived in Italy, and I brought this recipe home with me to Ireland and infused some Irish into it! The whiskey and honey ice cream is deliciously sweet with a subtle kick from the whiskey. It's a great dessert to serve after any main course.

1 Start by making the ice cream: Place a saucepan over medium heat and pour in the milk, cream, and vanilla extract. Bring to a boil and then reduce the heat to a simmer.

2 In a bowl, beat together the egg yolks and honey until pale and light.

3 Remove the milk and cream from the heat and, using a wire whisk, beat into the egg and honey mixture.

4 Let cool completely, then stir in the whiskey. Churn the mixture in an ice-cream maker according to the manufacturer's directions.

5 When ready to serve, place a scoop of the ice cream in a heatproof glass and pour over 3 tablespoons plus 1 teaspoon espresso coffee per serving. As the ice cream starts to melt instantly, I would recommend putting the ice cream in the glasses and bringing the pot of coffee to the table, then pouring the hot coffee over the ice cream in front of your lucky guests.

Serves 12

2½ cups freshly brewed
   espresso coffee

For the whiskey and honey ice
   cream
1¼ cups whole milk
1¼ cups heavy cream
1 teaspoon vanilla extract
5 large egg yolks
¾ cup plus 2 tablespoons
   golden honey
¼ cup Irish whiskey

You will need an ice-cream maker
and 12 heatproof glasses.

Baileys Irish Soda Bread *Ice Cream*

In any Irish kitchen there is always a stale piece of soda bread left over in the breadbin, which is a great excuse to make soda bread ice cream. Roasting the bread crumbs with the brown sugar creates little crunchy speckles throughout. The Baileys adds another depth of coffee and caramel flavor and a silky texture. You can leave this out if you prefer, but it really is delicious.

1 Preheat the oven to 350°F.

2 In a bowl, place the bread crumbs and brown sugar and mix well. Then sprinkle the sugared bread crumbs onto a baking sheet and spread out evenly. Bake in the oven for about 10 minutes, or until the bread crumbs are slightly darker and the sugar has melted. Stir occasionally while they are baking. Once the bread crumbs are baked, let cool.

3 Meanwhile, pour the milk and cream into a saucepan, place over medium heat, and stir in the white sugar. Using a small, sharp knife, slit the vanilla bean down its length and scoop out the tiny black seeds. Stir them into the milk and cream mixture. Reduce the heat and continue to stir, until all the sugar has dissolved, then remove from the heat.

4 In a large mixing bowl, lightly beat the eggs yolks. Gradually add the warm milk and cream mixture, beating gently to combine. Transfer the mixture back to the pan and place over low heat. Cook, stirring continuously, until the mixture thickens to the consistency of custard.

5 Remove the custard from the heat and stir in the Baileys, along with the cooled sugared bread crumbs. Mix well.

6 Pour the ice cream mixture into a freezerproof container, and freeze overnight before serving. Stir the ice cream two or three times to prevent it freezing into a solid block.

This will keep in the freezer for up to 1 month.

Makes 20 fl. oz

5oz bread crumbs from Irish soda bread (the bread should be at least 1 day old)
1/3 cup packed light brown sugar
1 cup milk
1 cup heavy cream
3/4 cup granulated sugar
1 vanilla bean
5 large free-range egg yolks
1/3 cup Baileys Irish cream liqueur

Preserving THE SEASONS

Preserving

How to Sterilize Jars

1 Set a large pot on the stovetop.

2 Check that your chosen jars have no chips or cracks.

3 Wash the jars and their lids thoroughly in hot soapy water. Rinse well and dry.

4 Place the jars right side up in the pot, cover completely with water, and bring to a boil over high heat.

5 Boil the jars for 15 minutes. Turn off the heat, add the lids and let sit for 10 minutes. Let cool the required amount (this varies according to the recipe– see below).

Putting your Preserves in Jars

1 Fill each jar with the preserve to within ¼ inch of the top of the jar.

2 Remove any air bubbles by poking the preserve in the jar with a skewer.

3 For non-liquid foods, it is important to remove any trapped air bubbles from the top–the easiest way to do this is to rub a knife along the top.

4 If the preserve is cool in temperature, it should be placed in a cooled sterilized jar. If the preserve is warm, it should be placed in a warm sterilized jar.

Testing that Jam is Set

1 Place a saucer in the freezer to chill, 10 minutes.

2 Remove from the freezer and place 1 teaspoon of the jam on the chilled saucer.

3 Push the jam back with your finger–if the jam wrinkles, it is set.

Tip: If you want to cut down on the sugar when making jam, substitute half the quantity with honey.

Wild Elderflower Cordial

Elderflower cordial is such a deliciously refreshing drink—for me it's the essence of an Irish summer, as it grows in abundance in the countryside hedgerows. Just mix one part cordial to two parts sparkling water. You can also use this cordial to make Wild Elderflower Jellies (page 223) and sorbets.

1 Gently rinse the elderflower heads and place them in a large bowl. Grate the lemon zest over the flowers, then slice the lemons and add them to the bowl.

2 Put the sugar in a saucepan with 2 quarts water and bring to a boil, stirring to ensure that the sugar dissolves. Take off the heat and let cool.

3 Once the syrup has cooled, pour it over the elderflowers and stir in the citric acid, if using. Cover with a clean kitchen towel and let infuse in the refrigerator for 24 hours.

4 Strain the cordial through a piece of cheesecloth and pour into sterilized glass bottles (see opposite).

This will keep for up to 1 month with citric acid; up to 1 week without.

Makes 2 quarts

30 heads elderflower
3 lemons
5 cups sugar
2 teaspoons citric acid (optional, but will keep the cordial preserved for up to 1 month)

You will need a piece of clean cheesecloth

For Sparkling Elderflower Cocktail, fill a Champagne flute with one part Wild Elderflower Cordial to two parts Prosecco or Champagne.

Gooseberry and Elderflower Jam

Tangy gooseberries simmered with sugar to sweeten, and elderflowers for a subtle floral flavor–so decadent! It's a heavenly jam that is delicious spooned over rice pudding, sandwiched in a Victoria sponge, or smothered on freshly baked scones with whipped cream. If you don't have elderflowers, just use elderflower cordial. Gooseberries are high in pectin so the jam will set quickly.

1 Put the gooseberries and sugar in a clean bowl and pour over 2½ cups water. Let steep overnight.

2 The next day, if using elderflower heads, rinse them in cold water and shake dry. Cut off the flowers with scissors, then put them onto the piece of cheesecloth, gather the sides together, and tie securely.

3 Transfer the gooseberries in their sugary water to a large saucepan, together with the elderflowers in their cheesecloth bag or the elderflower cordial. Stir gently over low heat until the sugar dissolves and the gooseberries are soft. Increase the heat to high and boil rapidly until setting point is reached–this should take about 15 minutes. Test it by spooning a little of the jam onto a cold saucer and pushing it with a spoon. If the jam wrinkles, it is set (see page 214).

4 Remove the pan from the heat, skim the film off the top of the jam, and discard the cheesecloth bag. Let cool slightly and then transfer to six warm sterilized jars (see page 214). Seal with the lids, label, and date.

The jam will keep for up to 6 months, stored in a cool, dry place.

Makes 6 (9-ounce) jars

3 pounds gooseberries, trimmed
6½ cups granulated sugar
2 heads elderflower or ¼ cup Wild
   Elderflower Cordial (see page 215)

If using elderflower heads, you will need a piece of clean cheesecloth

Summer Berry and Vanilla *Jam*

This is a perfect way to savor the flavors of summer in the fall months. The sweet summer berries are delicious with the subtle flavor of vanilla. Once you have used the vanilla pod, don't discard it–instead, dry it off and place it in the center of a jar of sugar. After it has infused for a few days, you will be left with beautiful vanilla sugar to use for syrups and baking. I love using mixed berries in this jam, but you could just use one type of berry, if you prefer.

1 In a saucepan, combine all of the ingredients and simmer over low heat, stirring every couple of minutes, until all the sugar is dissolved, about 15 minutes.

2 Turn up the heat and bring to a boil. Let boil until the jam begins to set (see page 214 for how to test the set of your jam). Remove the vanilla bean.

3 Pour the hot jam into six warm sterilized jars (see page 214) and let cool. Cover each with a disk of wax paper and seal with the lid.

The jam will keep for up to 3 months in a cool, dry place.

Makes about 6 (9-ounce) jars

2¼ pounds summer berries
  (e.g. raspberries, strawberries,
  blackberries, red currants,
  loganberries)
5 cups granulated sugar
1 vanilla bean, slit lengthwise

Fall Irish Compote

This is a delicious taste of fall in Ireland. Great served with yogurt and granola for breakfast, it's also perfect served with meats such as pork or game.

1 Start by making a syrup: In a saucepan over high heat, combine the sugar, star anise, and cinnamon with 2 cups water. Bring to a boil, stirring continuously, then reduce the heat and simmer for 5 minutes.

2 Next, stir in the apples and let cook for 10 minutes. The apples should be starting to get a bit soft by the end of the 10 minutes. Now stir in the blackberries and continue to cook until the compote is thick—this should take about another 10 minutes. As you stir, use the back of the spoon to break down the fruit.

3 Just before you jar the compote, discard the star anise and cinnamon. Let the compote cool, then pour it into eight cool sterilized jars (see page 214) and seal with the lids.

The compote will keep for up to 1 month in a cool, dry place.

Makes about 8 (9-ounce) jars

1 cup superfine sugar
1 star anise
1 cinnamon stick
26 ounces baking apples, peeled, cored, and coarsely chopped
2 cups blackberries

Blackberry and Apple *Jam*

I have a lovely memory of myself and my brother cycling alongside my sisters, while they walked carrying buckets to gather wild blackberries from the hedgerows. We would be wobbling on our bikes with one hand gripping the bike, and the other hand desperately trying to grab a blackberry from the buckets—I always knew I was going to be a skilled eater! We would arrive home with big purple smiles, and the sweet, juicy, plump blackberries were such a treat. My mum would take the blackberries and turn them into pots of jam, cooking them with apple, and we would have this on toast after our porridge every morning during the winter. It's the simple traditions that are the most special. I try to make a few pots every year, keeping this memory and tradition alive. It's one of my favorite jams.

1 In a heavy-bottomed saucepan, combine the apples with 1 cup water. Cover and simmer over low heat for 10 minutes. Add the blackberries and lemon zest and then stir in the sugar, continuing to stir until it has dissolved.

2 Bring to a boil and keep boiling until the jam begins to set (see page 214 for how to test the set of your jam).

3 Pour the hot jam into warm sterilized jars (see page 214) and let cool, then cover each with a disk of wax paper and seal with the lid. Store in a cool, dry place for up to 3 months.

The jam will keep for up to 3 months in a cool, dry place.

Makes about 6 (9-ounce) jars

1 pound baking apples, peeled, cored, and coarsely chopped
3½ cups blackberries
zest of 1 lemon
5 cups granulated sugar

Old-fashioned *Whiskey* Marmalade

There is nothing like a jar of old-fashioned whiskey marmalade served alongside Irish butter and toasted soda bread. Every house in Ireland has a pot in the cupboard at some stage. The tanginess of the Seville oranges with the sweetness of the Irish whiskey is utterly delicious! Traditionally, this would be made in Irish kitchens in January, as that's when the Seville oranges would arrive from Spain.

Makes 6 (8-ounce) jars

5 large (2¼ pounds) Seville oranges
juice of 2 lemons
5 cups gelling sugar
2¼ cups packed dark brown sugar
²/₃ cup Irish whiskey

You will need a large piece of cheesecloth

1 Cut the oranges into quarters. Using a sharp knife, carefully cut the orange flesh away from the peel, ensuring that you leave all the white pith behind. Cut the orange flesh into thin slices and place in a bowl.

2 Using a sharp fruit knife (or small knife), scrape off and discard all the membrane and pith from the peel. Then cut the peel into very thin slivers and place in a saucepan with 2 quarts water. Bring to a boil, then reduce the heat to a simmer and cook until the peel is very tender, about 2 hours.

3 Add the lemon juice to the orange flesh in the bowl. Place in the piece of cheesecloth, gather the sides together like a bag, and tie at the top. Tie the cheesecloth bag to the handle of a saucepan and let the bag dangle inside the pan so that all the juices are collected. Let drain for a couple of hours.

4 Squeeze all the remaining juices from the cheesecloth bag into the saucepan and discard the bag. Stir the white and brown sugars into the pan, along with the orange peel mixture, and place the saucepan over low heat, stirring occasionally, until all the sugar is dissolved. This should take about 15 minutes.

5 Remove from the heat and stir in the Irish whiskey. Let the marmalade cool for 20 minutes, then spoon into warm sterilized jars (see page 214). Cool completely, then seal with a lid.

The marmalade will keep for up to 1 month in a cool, dry place.

Mint and Red Currant *Jelly*

This combination of red currants and fresh mint is the perfect condiment to serve with roast lamb. There is a great tradition in Irish cuisine to make this jelly and serve it with mid-summer lamb, as the lamb is full of flavor at that time of the year and can take the sweetness of the red currants. It's also great whisked into gravy to add extra flavor and depth.

1 In a medium-size saucepan, place the red currants and whole sprigs of mint and cover with 4¼ cups cold water. Bring to a boil and then reduce the heat to low. Simmer for 15 minutes.

2 Remove the saucepan from the heat and let cool for about 10 minutes. Carefully pour the red currant mixture into the piece of cheesecloth, gather the sides together like a bag, and tie at the top. Tie the bag to the handle of a saucepan and let the bag dangle inside the pan so that all the juices are collected. Let drain for a couple of hours.

3 Squeeze out all the remaining juices from the cheesecloth bag into the saucepan and discard the bag. Stir in the sugar and lemon juice and place the saucepan over low heat, stirring occasionally, until all the sugar is dissolved. This will take about 15 minutes.

4 Remove the saucepan from the heat and stir in the chopped mint. Let the jelly cool for 20 minutes and then spoon into the warm sterilized jars (see page 214). Cool completely, then seal with a lid.

The jelly will keep for up to 1 month in a cool, dry place.

Makes 4 (8-ounce) jars

2¼ pounds red currants
2 sprigs of mint
5 cups granulated
     sugar
juice of 1 lemon
20 mint leaves, chopped

You will need a large piece of clean cheesecloth

Apple and Golden Raisin *Chutney*

When I had a stall at the farmers' markets in County Cork many years ago, I used to make and sell this chutney to go along with the pâté that I also sold. The apples get slowly cooked down, infused with spices, ginger, and golden raisins. It is so easy to make—all the work is in the gathering of the ingredients, and after that it's just stir and smile! This chutney is delicious with pâté, hard cheeses, and cold meats. I also use it to marinade a joint of pork.

Makes about 12 (9-ounce) jars

5½ tablespoons butter
4½ pounds baking apples, peeled,
   cored, and coarsely chopped
3 onions, peeled and finely chopped
2¾ cups light brown sugar
3 cups golden raisins
4½-inch piece fresh ginger, peeled
   and grated
3 teaspoons mustard seeds
2½ cups cider vinegar
sea salt and freshly ground
   black pepper

1 In a large saucepan over low heat, melt the butter. Stir in the apples and onions, cover, and cook for 5 minutes.

2 Remove the lid and stir in the brown sugar, golden raisins, fresh ginger, mustard seeds, and cider vinegar. Season with salt and black pepper. Mix well, then cover the pan, increase the heat, and bring to a boil. Reduce the heat and let simmer over medium heat for 20 minutes, stirring every 5 minutes.

3 After 20 minutes, remove the lid, reduce the heat more, and let cook until the apple has broken down and the chutney has turned a rich golden brown, another 20 minutes. Use the back of a wooden spoon to crush up the apples. Remove from the heat and let cool. The chutney will thicken more as it cools.

4 Once the chutney has cooled, spoon it into 12 cold, sterilized jars (see page 214). Cover with a disk of greaseproof or waxed paper and a lid, and label and date the jars.

The chutney will keep for up to 1 month in a cool, dry place.

Garden Tomato *Chutney*

Last year I planted about 6 tomato plants in a raised bed in the garden of our family home. Every week when I came home to visit I would go out to see if they had started to grow, but week after week there was nothing. Then, all in a matter of weeks, a glut of tomatoes sprouted from the plants and we were left with a huge basketful! We made salads, salsas, and tarts, but still had so many leftover that were about to go bad. So we decided to make this big pot of tomato chutney. It's a sweet chutney with a kick from the ginger and chile, and it's delicious with hard cheeses, cold meats, and burgers.

1 In a food processor, place the tomatoes, ginger, chile, and red bell pepper and blend until smooth.

3 Place a large saucepan over medium heat and pour in the blended tomato and ginger mixture. Then stir in the onion, apple, brown sugar, and cider vinegar and season with salt and black pepper. Bring to a boil, then reduce the heat and simmer until the chutney has started to thicken, about 40 minutes.

4 Let cool, then spoon into six cold, sterilized jars (see page 214). Cover with a disk of greaseproof or waxed paper and a lid, and label and date the jars.

The chutney will keep for up to 1 month in a cool, dry place.

Makes about 6 (9-ounce) jars

2¾ pounds ripe tomatoes, peeled
2-inch piece fresh ginger, peeled
  and grated
1 red chile, halved and seeded
1 red bell pepper, seeded and
  coarsely chopped
1 onion, peeled and diced
7 ounces baking apples, peeled,
  cored, and coarsely chopped
1 cup light brown sugar
¾ cup plus 1 tablespoon cider
  vinegar
sea salt and freshly ground
  black pepper

Spiced Cranberry Sauce

Although not strictly a preserve, this spiced cranberry sauce offers such a great flavor of its season. Perfect with Christmas dishes.

Serves 6

1 cup granulated sugar
8 whole cloves
1-inch piece fresh ginger, peeled
4 cups fresh cranberries
1 cinnamon stick
1 red chile, slit lengthwise and seeded

1 Place the sugar in a saucepan with ½ cup water and slowly bring to a boil. Once the sugar has dissolved, lower the heat.

2 Stick the cloves into the fresh ginger and place in the saucepan, followed by the cranberries, cinnamon stick, and chile. Let simmer until the cranberries have popped, about 15 minutes.

3 When the cranberries have popped, the sauce is ready. Serve the spicy cranberry and orange sauce with a goose or my Traditional Irish Christmas Turkey (page 162).

Cucumber *Pickle*

This is delicious with the Poached Whole Salmon on page 156.

1 Place all of the ingredients in a ceramic or glass bowl and mix together well. Cover and let pickle in the refrigerator for 2 hours. Take it out every 30 minutes and give it a stir.

This will keep in the fridge for 2 weeks.

Serves 6

2 cucumbers, very thinly sliced
1 onion, thinly sliced
¾ cup granulated sugar
1 cup cider vinegar
2 teaspoons yellow mustard seeds
1 teaspoon salt

Honey and Apple Salad Dressing

This simple dressing works with most salads, and is full of crisp, fresh flavors.

1 Place all of the ingredients in a ceramic or glass bowl and beat together using a fork or small wire whisk. Season with salt and black pepper to taste and drizzle over your chosen salad.

Serves 6

1 teaspoon Dijon mustard
1 teaspoon golden honey
2 tablespoons apple cider vinegar
zest of 1 lemon
6 tablespoons extra virgin olive oil

Occasions

I confess I love tablescaping as much as I love cooking…

And that's a lot. If you haven't heard of the word "tablescaping" before, let me explain. It's basically creating a beautiful landscape on your table from place settings to floral arrangements. For me the table can set the tone for the evening.

It can be as simple as wrapping a sprig of fresh rosemary around a napkin or pebbles gathered from the beach used as place names or using some nice paper or postcards on which to write individual menus. I love to be dictated by what's in season to kick start my creativity. Fruits can be such great centerpieces and also handy for holding place cards holders. Pomegranates, figs, lemons, ornamental squashes, apples, can all be used as place name holders, just cut a slit on the top of the fruit and slip the card into the slit. Also follow what flowers, colors and mood of the time of year and keep it simple by avoiding conflicting patterns in the tablecloth and napkins and by using the same type or color of flowers. Try to match the accessories to the occasion, whether this is festive, glamorous, romantic or magical. At Christmas, for example, what could be easier than taking a piece of ribbon and tying a name card to the back of each guest's chair with a sprig of holly? Or, for spring, pick a few daffofils and tie one on each napkin with a yellow ribbon. If you are looking for a dried flower to add to the table, lavender is always fantastic.

The delighted look on a guest's face when I bring them to my table that I have tablescaped is worth every inch of effort. Life is about creating "moments" that we will cherish forever, and most of my golden moments or memories happen around a dinner table because that's my favorite place to be—and did I mention that it's so much fun! I usually do my tablescaping as much as I can the night before, so that I can enjoy the process without feeling rushed.

Valentine's Day Menu

Starter

CARPACCIO OF IRISH BEEF
WITH AGED COOLEA CHEESE (page 129)

or

ARTICHOKE AND KNOCKALARA CHEESE SOUFFLÉ (page 113)

Main Course

LOBSTER WITH DILL WEED GNOCCHI,
SEA BEANS AND BROWN BUTTER (page 143)

or

VENISON, CHILE, AND CHOCOLATE STEW (page 148)

Dessert

IRISH AFFOGATO WITH WHISKEY AND HONEY ICE CREAM
(page 208)

or

IRISH COFFEE CHOCOLATE MOUSSE (page 207)

Valentine's *Tablescape*

LINEN

I am not a fan of red linen on Valentine's day, as I don't think red is a very relaxing color. I prefer to go with cream – it's a soft, romantic color and works very well by candlelight. You could scatter silver or pale pink heart-shaped confetti around the table for an instant Valentine setting.

FLOWERS

Try and source soft, delicate flowers to complement the cream linen setting. Snowdrops, primroses and crocuses are absolutely beautiful and would work so well for a Valentine's dinner floral display. If you only have a few flowers, place one or two sprigs in small, pretty bottles scattered around the table.

POETIC NOTE

Write a short romantic poem from Keats or Shelley on a piece of nice paper. Roll up a linen napkin and wrap the poem around the nakin, and tie it together using a pretty ribbon. Place this on the side plate.

> *See, the mountains kiss high heaven,*
> *And the waves clasp one another;*
> *No sister flower could be forgiven*
> *If it disdained its brother;*
> *And the sunlight clasps the earth,*
> *And the moonbeams kiss the sea;–*
> *What are all these kissings worth,*
> *If thou kiss not me?*
>
> PERCY BYSSHE SHELLEY

VALENTINE'S TREE CENTREPIECE

Place a large wooden branch in a vase and hang heart-shaped decorations off the small sprigs to create a Valentine's tree for the center of the table.

I LOVE YOU PEBBLES

Take three pebbles for each place settings. Write "I" on the first pebble, "love" on the second pebble, and "you" on the third. Place them at the top of the place settings, in front of where the main course plate will be placed.

VINTAGE BOTTLES & JARS

Spread lots of vintage bottles and jars around the dinner table and fill them with tea lights or, if they have a thin neck, place candlesticks in them. The more varied the heights of the candles, the better.

VALENTINE'S COCKTAIL TRAY

Set up a retro cocktail tray in your living room to have a pre-dinner drink, such as the Pomegranate Cocktail, below. If you don't have a nice silver tray, simply line your tray with a linen napkin or retro doilies.

Pomegranate cocktail

INGREDIENTS:
crushed ice
pomegranate juice
Prosecco
ginger ale
pomegranate seeds
brandy (optional)

Fill a glass halfway with crushed ice, then add two parts pomegranate juice to two parts Prosecco and one part ginger ale. Add about 5 pomegranate seeds, plus a splash of brandy if you wish.

St Patrick's Day Menu

Starters

GRAVLAX WITH DILL WEED AND JUNIPER BERRIES (page 123)

or

COLCANNON SOUP WITH PARSLEY PESTO (page 70)

Main Course

WILD NETTLE GNOCCHI WITH
CASHEL BLUE SAUCE (page 134)

or

CRISPY CHICKEN WITH A CREAMY IRISH WHISKEY
AND WILD MUSHROOM SAUCE (page 144)

Dessert

SALTED CARAMEL WHISKEY BREAD AND BUTTER PUDDING
WITH GOLDEN RAISINS (page 194)

or

GUINNESS CAKE (page 40)

St Patrick's *Ideas for Decorating*

St Patrick's Day is celebrated on 17th March, and is an important public holiday in Ireland. It's traditionally associated with the color green, so I like to extend that theme to the table by creating a stunning and beautifully scented herb table runner.

How to create *an Herb Table Runner*

YOU WILL NEED:
- pieces of green water-retaining foam—how many depends on how long your table is. On average you would need 3 to 5 blocks.
- Eucalyptus, bay leaf stems and green foliage
- Herbs, such as thyme, rosemary, sage, and marjoram
- 2 to 3 thyme, sage, or rosemary plants
- Candlesticks or holders

1. Start by soaking your foam in water. I recommend filling a basin of water and allowing the foam to soak in it for one minute. Don't leave it for any longer, because if the foam is over watered it will break. As well as keeping the fresh leaves and herbs in place, this soaked foam will keep them watered and looking fresh.

2. Place the watered pieces of foam on a plastic container (they usually come with the foam) or on wooden boards. Line them up down the center of your table, leaving gaps in between for the plants.

3. Place the thyme, sage, or rosemary plants in the gaps between the pieces of foam.

4. Place your candlesticks or holders on top of the pieces of foam, in the center.

5. Cut your eucalyptus and foliage into 6-inch stems and set aside.

6. Begin with the sides: Stick sprigs of ecalyptus into the foam, followed by herbs and bay leaf stems, then foliage leaves along the sides at an angle, until you are unable to see the foam.

7. Then move on to the top of the foam. Stick the remaining stems of eucalytus, herbs, bay leaf stems, and foliage in the center. Try not to display it too perfectly, placing different heights along the way.

CHAIR HERB DECORATION

Gather together four stems of herbs (rosemary, sage, thyme, and a bay leaf) all cut to about 5 to 6 inches in length. Tie them together using a piece of twine at the base of the stem, and leaving enough twine left to tie the bunch onto the back of the table.

PLACE SETTINGS

The rustic, natural beauty of this table display is beautifully complemented by keeping place settings really simple. A neutral-colored napkin can act as a placemat, while a simple piece of card stamped with a tree or plant design makes an understated name card.

Easter/Spring Menu

Starter

POTTED DINGLE CRAB (page 125)

or

NETTLE AND WILD GARLIC SOUP (page 75)

Main Course

CREAMY FENNEL AND TURBOT GRATIN (page 95)

or

SUMMER LAMB WITH FENNEL AND
ROASTED NECTARINES (page 147)

Dessert

RHUBARB AND GINGER CHEESECAKE (page 193)

or

WILD ELDERFLOWER GELATIN DESSERTS (page 202)

Easter *Tablescape*

EASTER EGG TREE

I create an Easter egg tree every year, both at home and at my restaurants. It's my table centerpiece for the weeks leading up to Easter and for my Easter lunch. Buy a big bunch of pussy willow branches (cherry blossoms would also be gorgeous) – you can pick these up at most flower shops. Place the branches in a glass vase and fill the base of the vase with shells (you could also use pebbles, or steal your kids marbles!) to keep the branches upright. From each branch, hang mini eggs tied on a ribbon. It looks so pretty – and on Easter Sunday, you can let your guests take a mini egg home from the tree!

Other ideas for your Easter Table

EASTER PLACE SETTINGS

Cut the stems of 20 fresh daffodils so that they are about 5 inches tall. Separate them into 4 bunches of 5 and tie each bunch with twine. Put the bunches into small glasses and place one in front of each place setting. Take 4 small cards (about the size of business cards) and write "Happy Easter" on each. Place the cards leaning on the glass of daffodils facing your guest.

EGG SHELL CANDLES

Break the top off an egg shell and carefully empty out the contents (you could use them for one of my Baked Eggs recipes on page 55). Rinse the egg shell carefully and place a small tea light inside. Pop the egg shell in an egg cup and arrange these beside each of the daffodil arrangements.

LINEN

For a fresh spring table, use a green or yellow-and-white gingham tablecloth. You can pick the material up cheaply in good household or material stores.

EASTER FLOWER ARRANGEMENT

A lovely idea for an Easter-themed floral arrangement is to place a cake stand or pretty tray in the center of the table and place 6 egg cups on top of it. Fill the egg cups with yellow tulips, daffodils or narcissus cut into 4-inch stems.

Sea Shore Menu

Starter

MUSSELS COOKED WITH CREAM, CHORIZO, GARLIC,
AND FLAT-LEAF PARSLEY (page 92)

or

SEAWEED AND VEGETABLE SALAD (page 87)

Main Course

CRAB CAKES WITH TARRAGON MAYONNAISE (page 119)

or

DILLISK RAVIOLI OF IRISH SMOKED SALMON AND GOAT
CHEESE WITH WATERCRESS PESTO (page 140)

Dessert

ROSE WATER-INFUSED CARRAGEEN MOSS
WITH RHUBARB COMPOTE (page 205)

or

BAILEYS IRISH SODA BREAD ICE CREAM (page 211)

Sea shore *Tablescape*

Living on an island, I am never far from the shore. There is an abundance of treasure to be foraged from the strands or beaches to make a naturally beautiful table. Even a simple runner of fresh seaweed down the center of the table, with seashells and tea lights scattered through the seaweed, can create a magical seascape.

How to create *The Seashore Tablescape*

YOU WILL NEED:

- Starfish
- Ferns, Feverfew, Wild Fennel or Sea Holly
- Vintage bottles of varying sizes
- Oyster shells
- Scallop shells
- Pieces of driftwood or branches
- Candlesticks or holders
- Cards for place markings
- Twine
- Paper tags (for menus)

STEPS

1. Start by choosing your linen. Grays, whites, soft blues, or tweed-style tablecoths will work beautifully.

2. Place your driftwood pieces or branches in the middle of the table, and place the vintage bottles on either side. Add a little water to each bottle and arrange the wild flowers and ferns in them.

3. Scatter starfish and/or scallop shells along the table.

4. For the place markings, fold pieces of card so they stand up, and glue a small starfish or flat shell on one of the upper corners.

5. Fill clean oyster shells with freshly ground black pepper, sea salt and butter. The oyster shells could also be used to serve salsa, mayonnaise, guacamole, or similar.

6. Roll your napkins up like a scroll, and wrap your handwritten or typed menu around the napkin. Tie together with twine, and finish with a tag with "Menu" written on it.

7. Use large scallop shells as side plates and place your scroll-style napkin and menu on top.

Christmas Menu

Starters

SMOKED MACKEREL AND DILLISK PÂTÉ WITH
FENNEL CRISPBREADS (page 115)

or

WILD MUSHROOM AND CHICKEN LIVER PÂTÉ (page 131)

Main Course

TRADITIONAL IRISH ROAST TURKEY WITH SAUSAGE, HERB AND
APPLE STUFFING AND SPICED CRANBERRY SAUCE
(pages 162–163 and 226)

or

CORK-SPICED BEEF WITH BEET AND HORSERADISH CREAM
(pages 164 and 177)

Dessert

TRADITIONAL IRISH CHRISTMAS PLUM PUDDING (page 43)

or

INDIVIDUAL RASPBERRY AND BAILEYS TRIFLES (page 206)

Christmas *Tablescape*

I am not a huge fan of tinsel, gold, or any kind of bold Christmas decorations. I prefer simpler place settings using cinnamon sticks, cedar, pine cones, etc. Even white snowflake decorations scattered on a white linen tablecloth and white candles with ivy looped around the stem of the candlesticks can look so elegant. My advice would be to keep it simple. Start with lovely, crisp, white table linen and add one or two of the ideas below, with lots of candles, either with the ivy, like I mention above, or small pillar candles in vases filled with cranberries.

SNOW-TIPPED PINE CONE PLACE SETTINGS

Pine cones are a really natural, easy and inexpensive way to decorate the Chrsitmas table. Using a hacksaw, cut a 1-inch slit down the middle of the pine cones. Then place the pine cones on a sheet of old newspaper and gently spray the tips of the cones with artifical snow spray. Leave them to dry for about 30 minutes. While they are drying, write your guests' names or the Christmas lunch menu on individual cards. Once the snow-tipped cones are dry, insert the name cards or menus into each slot, making sure that you can see all the written name or menu.

CHRISTMAS TREE PLACE SETTINGS

Cut 4-inch sprigs off your Christmas tree, one for each guest. Then use either the base of a tea light candle (cutting off the wick), or a clementine, insert the Christmas tree sprig into the center, so that the sprig stands upright and creates a mini tree. Place one on each table setting, and pop a name card on the top of each tree. You could also leave it without a name card, as they will also look great with a small piece of ribbon tied on the top in a bow.

CINNAMON NAPKIN BUNDLES

Roll your napkins into a neat bundle and set aside. Take two cinnamon sticks per table setting and tie them together using a pretty ribbon, leaving enough ribbon to wrap around the napkin. Then place the ribbon-tied cinnamon sticks around the napkin, cinnamon sticks facing up, and tie the ribbon in a bow.

CEDAR-LEAVED CHARGER PLATES

Place the cedar leaves (allow three per guest) about 8 to 10 inches in length on a sheet of old newspaper and gently spray with artifical snow spray. Leave them to dry for about 30 minutes. Then take a charger or an old plate that's larger that your main course plate and arrange on the table where you plan on seating each guest. If you have neither a charger nor an old plate, don't worry—work directly on the table. Place about three snow-sprayed cedar leaves on each place setting or charger, and distribute them evenly so that you have a circle of snowy cedar leaves. Any color plate placed on top will look so festive and pretty.

DRIED ORANGE SLICES

A few weeks before Christmas, slice a few oranges about ½ inch thick, place them on a baking tray lined with parchment paper and place in your oven on its lowest heat setting for about an hour, or until they have completely dried out. These can be used for a number of things. String a pretty ribbon through the center of a dried orange slice and use it to tie it around a rolled napkin or off a Christmas tree. You can also just scatter them around the table, as they look so pretty. I have an open fire, and every year I fill a basket with these dried orange slices and cinnamon sticks, and every hour or so on Christmas Day I throw them into the fire to let off a beautiful festive scent.

While many of these Irish producers and suppliers ship to the States, those that do not I've still included in the hope that you'll find yourself in Ireland one day and can bring some of it back with you!

Cheesemongers

NEAL'S YARD DAIRY
UK-based suppliers of a number of the cheeses I use, including Coolea, Cashel Blue and Ardrahan, with weekly shipments to the US.
www.nealsyarddairy.co.uk

SHERIDAN'S CHEESEMONGER
Artisan cheesemongers with stores in Dublin, Galway, Waterford and Meath plus an online shop, which delivers to the US. They stock a variety of the cheeses used in this book, including Bellingham Blue, Cashel Blue, Coolea, Cooleeney, Crozier Blue, Desmond, Gubbeen, Hegarty's and St Tola.
www.sheridanscheesemongers.com
0033469245110

SIX FORKS CHEESE
Raleigh, NC-based cheese shop that carries many brands of Irish cheese.
www.sixforkcheese.com

Food Stores

AVOCA
Wide range of Irish artisan produce. A selection of stores nationwide in Ireland, and delivers to the US.
www.avoca.com

ARDKEEN QUALITY FOOD STORE
Supermarket stocking a wide range of Irish artisan produce, and delivers to the US.
www.ardkeen.com

Dairy Producers

ARDSALLAGH GOATS CHEESE
Soft, hard and smoked goats cheese Produced by the Murphy Family in County Cork.
www.ardsallaghgoats.com

BANDON VALE
Cheeses ranging from cheddars to Emmental.
www.bandonvale.ie

BELLINGHAM BLUE
Blue cheese made from raw cows milk cheese. Produced by Peter and Anita Thomas in County Louth.
www.bellingham.ie

BLUEBELL FALLS GOATS CHEESE
Soft goats cheese. Produced by the O'Sullivan family in County Cork.
www.bluebellfalls.com

CARRIGBYRNE
Semi soft camembert-style cows milk cheese. Produced by the Berridge family in County Wexford.
www.carrigbyrne.ie

CASHEL & CROZIER BLUE
Both blue cheese, Cashel made from cows milk and Crozier made from sheeps milk. Produced by the Grubb family in County Tipperary.
www.cashelblue.com

COOLEA
Gouda-style aged cows milk cheese. Produced by the Willem family in County Cork, available through Sheridans and Neal's Yard.
www.cooleacheese.com

DURRUS
Semi-soft cows raw milk cheese. Produced by Jeffa Gill in County Cork
www.durruscheese.com

GLENILEN
Butter, yogurts, creams and desserts made from their own cows milk. Produced by the Kingston family in County Cork.
www.glenilenfarm.com

GUBBEEN
Semi soft cows milk cheese. Produced by the Ferguson family in County Cork. Available widely in the US through Neal's Yard.
www.gubbeen.com

KNOCKALARA
Produced by Agnes and Wolfgang Schliebitz and sold in local stores and at Dungarvan Farmers' Market. If you can't buy it, a good-quality feta makes a good substitute.

TOONSBRIDGE DAIRY
Ricotta and mozzarella made from buffalo milk.
Produced by Toby Simmonds and Johnny Lynch using mill from their herd of water buffalo in County Cork.
www.therealoliveco.com

Fish

With fish, it's best to always go for fresh— for example, I get the fish for my restaurant from The Quay Fish Shop in Dun Laoghaire, a 5-minute drive away. There are some great Irish producers of smoked salmon—some are listed below, and you can ask your local fishmonger.

BURREN SMOKEHOUSE
Organic smoked salmon, sold through their website.
www.burrensmokehouse.ie

UMMERA SMOKEHOUSE
Smoked salmon, as well as chicken, bacon and duck. Produced by Anthony Creswell in Country Cork and sold worldwide through the website.
www.ummera.com

WOODCOCK SMOKERY
Specialists in slow-smoked, wild-caught fresh fish. Sold through Sheridans, Neal's Yard and their own website.
www.woodcocksmokery.com

Meat

GUBBEEN
Salamis, hams, bacon and sausages. Produced by Fingal Ferguson in County Cork
www.gubbeen.com

FOOD IRELAND
Online suppliers of sausages, blood puddings, and more.
www.foodireland.com

KRAWACZYK'S WEST CORK SALAMIS
Produced by Frank Krawaczyk in County Cork
frank@ocean.free.net

McGEOUGHS BUTCHERS
Air-dry cured lamb, pork and beef.
Camp Street, Oughterard, County Galway
www.connemarafinefoods.ie

O'FLYNN'S BUTCHERS
36 Marlborough Street, Cork City, County Cork
Tel: 00 353 (0)21 427 5685

TOM DURCAN BUTCHERS
Spiced beef and a full butcher's counter.
www.tomdurcanmeats.ie

Preserves

All the following Preserves suppliers ship to the US.

HIGHBANK ORCHARD SYRUP
This syrup is made from apples grown at Highbank farm in Kilkenny. Described as Ireland's answer to maple syrup, it's used in my Summer Lamb recipe on page 147. It's sold at Selfridges and a number of independent stores. It is also available through the producer's website.
www.highbankorchards.com

MILEEVEN HONEY
Pure Irish honey and other preserves produced by the Gough family in County Kilkenny.
www.mileevenfinefoods.com

THE APPLE FARM
Pure apple juices from the farm produced by the Trass family in County Tipperary.
www.theapplefarm.com

WILD ABOUT
Handmade chutneys, syrups, cocktail bases and pesto. Produced by the Falconer family in County Wexford
www.wildabout.ie

Seaweeds

THE CORNISH SEAWEED COMPANY
Producers of sea spaghetti, Carrageen moss (also called 'sea moss' and dillisk (also called 'dulse'). Available at Whole Foods, health stores and their own website.
www.cornishseaweedcompany.co.uk

IRISH SEAWEEDS
Online supplier of a variety of seaweeds and similar ingredients, including Carrageen moss. Ships to the US.
www.irishseaweeds.com

ON THE WILD SIDE
Irish Seaweed based produce Produced by Olivier Beaujouan
seatoland@hotmail.com

PRANNIE RHATIGAN
The queen of Irish Seaweed! Her website is great for everything seaweed related.
www.prannie.com

WILD IRISH SEA VEG
Produced by the Talty family in County Clare.
www.wildirishseaveg.com

Bakery

DITTY'S OAT CAKES
Artisan Bakery. Produced by Robert Ditty in Northern Ireland, and available in the US. Check their website.
www.dittysbakery.com

Sea Salt

ATLANTIC SEA SALT
Produced by the O'Neill Family in County Cork.
www.irishatlanticsalt.ie

ACHILL ISLAND SEA SALT
Produced by the O'Malley Family in Achill Island, County Mayo.
www.achillislandseasalt.ie

Rapeseed Oil

BROIGHTER GOLD RAPESEED OIL
Produced by the Kane Family in County Monaghan.
www.broightergold.co.uk

DONEGAL RAPESEED OIL
Produced by the Duignan family in County Donegal.
www.donegalrapeseedoilco.com

Websites

FOR INFORMATION ON IRISH FOOD

www.slowfoodireland.ie
www.guides.ie
www.bordbia.ie
www.craftbutchers.ie
www.irishseedsavers.ie
www.irelandmarkets.ie
www.irishbeekeeping.ie
www.goodfoodireland.ie

And me...
www.clodaghmckenna.com

Index

Acknowledgments

My first and biggest thank you is to Kyle Cathie. You are a woman that I look up to in so many ways. You have given me so many opportunities, and have allowed me to make yet another dream come true with this book. I am forever thankful.

For Tara O'Sullivan, the editor, you are one of the kindest people I have ever worked with, and I mean that from my heart. Your gentle way is something of a treasure in this world we live in, always encouraging, always forgiving (of my lateness!), and you cared so much for this book. You have been a fantastic editor, and gathered the most wonderful team. To Tara Fisher, the photographer, I am in awe of your eye. I could spend hours in your company and still be surprised at your talent. You captured the story and love that I have for every recipe in this book, thank you so much for all the energy and dedication you gave. To the magical food stylists Annie Rigg and Kathryn Bruton, you are so creative, and your beautiful talent will bring me (and everyone else!) joy every time I open the pages of this book, thank you. To Wei Tang, the prop stylist, thank you for gathering the most beautiful treasures to place my food on—you have captured Irish style as I see it. To sweet Fiona Barry, make up artist, how lovely are you, thank you for my glow! To the proofreader, Corinne Masciocchi, thank you for your attention to details. To the designer, Lucy Gowans, and the production team, Nic Jones and Gemma John, the layout is so beautiful, thank you.

To my family—my mum for endless cups of tea and words of encouragement while I strived to make my deadline, and to my sister Mairead for keeping me focused and for endless phone conversations! To my sister Niamh, who is always a style inspiration, and my brother Jim, who gives me endless encouragement. And to my sister-in-law

Erin, who has worked with me now for 8 years—I am not sure what I would do without you. And my nieces and nephews, who are as excited about this book as I am, I love you so much.

To all the team at Clodagh's Kitchen restaurants, thank you for all your support while I wrote this book, especially Michael Andrews, Georgina Collier and Kamil Pekar.

Thank you to my agent John Ferriter, for believing in this book and me!

And most of all thank you to my love, Peter Gaynor, who loves everything that I cook—even if it's a disaster.